STREETWEAR

STREET WEAR
The Insider's Guide
Steven Vogel

CHRONICLE BOOKS
SAN FRANCISCO

Library of Congress Cataloging-in-Publication
Data available.

ISBN-10: 0-8118-6036-1
ISBN-13: 978-0-8118-6036-9

Manufactured in China

Book design by Samuel Clark
Cover design by Adam Machacek

Distributed in Canada by Raincoast Books
9050 Shaughnessy Street
Vancouver, British Columbia V6P 6E5

10 9 8 7 6 5 4 3 2 1

Chronicle Books LLC
680 Second Street
San Francisco, CA 94107

www.chroniclebooks.com

CONTENTS

INTRODUCT

The word 'street', used with another noun such as 'wear' or 'culture', is currently being used by so many different people and institutions to describe so many different things, that for two decades it has been almost impossible to find a single appropriate definition for it.

But most agree that streetwear is at the core of an intensely independent urban subculture. Over the past thirty years, it has been one of the most widely seen and quickly embraced public expressions of street culture in general.

Not everything worn on the street is automatically streetwear, and neither is there a uniform code of clothing that makes streetwear what it is. Yet there is an unspoken understanding between those who wear streetwear and are involved in the subculture about what it is, or perhaps more specifically, what it is not. Confusing? Yes.

Even though this book is intended to give readers an insight into the history, future and content of streetwear, it does not include a blueprint of which brands are 'street'. Nor will you find the final word on where to buy streetwear or how you should wear it. Instead, *Streetwear* offers opinions, statements, short stories and interviews from, and with, those who reflect, live and are the very essence of streetwear.

Rather than representing a set of brands or clothes, *Streetwear* represents a lifestyle that many agree was born in the early 1980s in New York. Due to the constant alienation and frustration felt mainly by inner city kids, not just in New York but worldwide, a community was formed that was influenced by skateboarding, punk, hardcore, reggae, hip hop, an emerging club culture, graffiti, travel and the art scene in downtown city centre areas.

The early days of streetwear were marked by a do-it-yourself attitude: clothes were chosen to suit a lifestyle which needed a mix of affordable and practical clothing, but that would also look good in clubs.

But streetwear pioneers were faced with a major problem: companies didn't make clothes specifically for this subculture. This was especially underlined when the Beastie Boys made their appearance on the world stage. Here was a group of young, white New Yorkers, previously unknown outside the New York punk/hardcore scene, but with their release *License to Ill*, turned the whole world upside down with their music and their appearance. Not only were they rapping on tour with Run DMC and Madonna, they looked totally distinct. Most people would agree that their music dramatically changed the musical landscape of the time. However, their impact on the ways in which people subsequently dressed was of equal importance. Following massive worldwide media coverage, the Beastie Boys succeeded in creating their own look: the look of urban kids from New York whose priorities were music, skateboarding, art and partying. The Beastie Boys offered a uniform to the world's disenfranchized kids (how many people can remember ripping VW emblems off cars and hanging them around their neck at some stage in their teenage years?).

But until a small group of like-minded individuals got together to make clothes for themselves and their friends, there was no one to provide the masses with this new look. These innovators opened the way for an industry to emerge which offered a common set of ideals and gave kids all over the world a place to work, a place to live and a place to be understood. In catering for streetwear aficionados and in drawing attention to the widespread desire for a new fashion, these pioneers stimulated the rise of a multi-billion dollar industry. And with that came the inevitably uglier aspects that any such large-scale industry seems to incur.

Despite, or perhaps because of this, it is the dual ideals of independence and a DIY ethic that have been carried forward from the early days of hip hop, skateboarding and punk to contemporary streetwear as we know it today. Large international companies can often get it wrong when it comes to designing, marketing and selling their own take on streetwear, precisely because there is no formula to make something 'street'. Instead, as this book hopes to demonstrate, streetwear is a combination of attitudes, aesthetics and activities that binds a group of people with similar interests together. It isn't something that can be analyzed from the outside, learned, reproduced and then packaged to be sold to the undeserving public. In order to be successfully involved in the streetwear industry, many would argue, including myself, that it is essential to have been a part of the subculture in the first place.

This book aims to give the reader insight into what streetwear means via interviews and short stories with those involved in the subculture from all around the world. By discussing streetwear with those who are truly immersed in it, these interviews should reveal what streetwear actually means, what it is, what it involves, who is involved, where it comes from, where it currently stands – and where it is going.

Certainly, not all those who could have contributed to this book are included. However, each individual or brand tells a personal story about a topic that is dear to me, and in creating this book, I hope to be able to give something back to a culture that has been my home and soul ever since I stepped on my first skateboard.

Steven Vogel

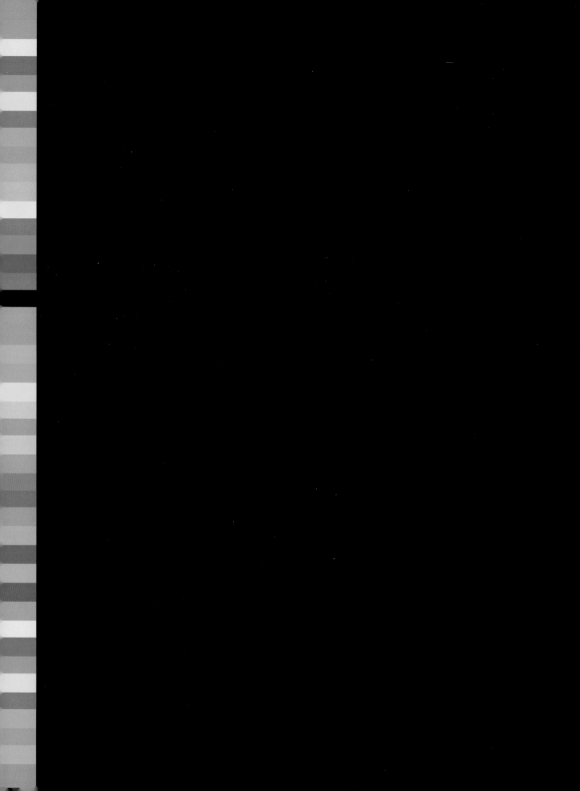

PART 1
DESIGN

▲ AKA x Nike ID Charity Auction Dunk Lo's

Founded by: **Allen Benedikt**
When: **1994/2005**
Where: **New York, USA**
Website: **www.akanyc.com**

Even a few years ago, just as graffiti was becoming mainstream, there were few publications about this art form. Bibles such as *Subway Art* and *Spraycan Art* existed, but they had already been around for fifteen years. There were also a few underground zines and websites, like Artcrimes.com, but if you wanted to know more about graffiti you had to really delve deep. One of the better zines was 12ozprophet.com, but as soon as graffiti exploded into the mainstream, the original pioneers and writers disappeared from view and graffiti became 'artified' and distorted. But graffiti has now reached a point where things need to change: in order to remain as vital and relevant today, it needs to reach back to purer roots. 12ozprophet has beckoned that call with a book that draws a

line, insisting simply that you either understand and recognize graffiti's importance, or you don't. Published in 2005, *"also known as"* became the new cornerstone in graffiti culture. After producing another graffiti-based publication with world-famous artist Krink and Alife NYC, "also known as" (AKA) quickly became an institution in itself. Allen Benedikt is the driving force behind AKA's creative whirlwind, and is inspiring the regeneration of graffiti.

Streetwear is a new term for something that most people either don't, or can't, define. Yet there seems to be a collective understanding about what it is. How do you define streetwear?
I see streetwear as a lifestyle brand that comes from, or is directed back towards, the street or street culture.

Credibility goes hand-in-hand with authenticity, and creative concepts and strong graphics generally go hand-in-hand with success. If you can add quality production to all that, you have a winning package.

When did you realize you were involved in something special and new?
There have been several moments that made me stop and realize that I was witnessing the emergence of something new: heading out to the ASR trade shows in the early 1990s with Don Busweiler, Jorge Cuartas and the rest of the Pervert Crew; watching GFS – Not From Concentrate change the landscape overnight with Philly's Blunt; listening to Shaun Stüssy explain the ins and outs of the game. Seeing an entirely new industry

▼ *"also known as"* (the book)

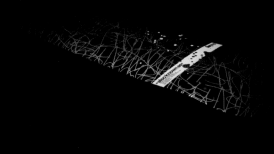

▲ Views of *"also known as"* (the book) during production

sprout up around the surf, skate and graffiti cultures. Milestones happen all the time.

Especially in clothing terms, what are streetwear's strengths and weaknesses?
The strengths lie in the rebellious nature of the mind set, as well as the culture's dynamic and elusive qualities. Weaknesses creep in when there's so much momentum that people and companies are scared to try something new. Everyone becomes so scared to stand in the shadow, or not be cool, that they appropriate the formula, instead of laying new ground. That's when shit becomes stale and boring.

Could you describe the most memorable events that inspired you, especially in terms of the impact you had on streetwear?
Watching Pervert go from being a concept and a few crack and peel stickers from Kinko's, to a huge hit, and then die into obscurity. Hanging out with everyone at an old reunion in Rock Steady Park and having Dondi (RIP) roll up on his bike with a big smile. Dropping by the Subware/Project Dragon

booth to meet Futura, Stash and Bleu (RIP) for the first time and finding out they were fans of the 12ozprophet zine. My week living with Os Gemeos in 1997, and watching their rise to success. Moving to Brooklyn and becoming good friends with my upstairs neighbour, Kaws. Having great dinners and discussions with Fraser Cooke and Giorgio de Mitri. Talking streetwear and business with David Oved (Akademiks), and streetwear and culture with Donwan (PRPS). Too many to mention.

The key to success is longevity. How do you apply this to yourself, and to your business?
The key to longevity is staying passionate, honest and dedicated. There's no doubt that everyone's going to face challenges along the way, but if you don't have at least these core qualities, you're not going to get through them in the long run.

Where do you think streetwear is going?
Who knows? It'll probably follow the same up and down cycles as everything else. Hopefully it stays fun and interesting along the way.

Recently, focus has shifted onto streetwear products. How do you explain that, and what do you think of this development?
I try not to think about it. I feel like I wasted a lot of effort trying to analyze the culture and its motives. It becomes obsessive, takes the fun out of the game, and leads to the same tired formulas that make the culture boring and the industry stale. Any asshole can swipe a graphic from popular culture, and drop it on a t-shirt to lock up with the latest sneaker colourways. It'd be a lot more fun for the producers and consumers if everyone would skip past the easy recipes for success and get back to innovating.

◀ *"also known as"* (the book)

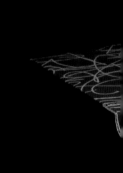

AKA Air Force Ones

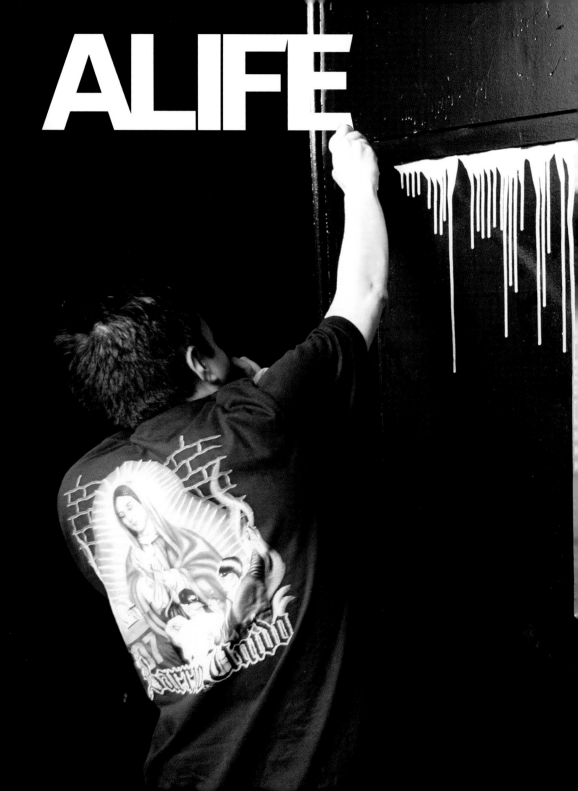

Founded by: **Arnaud Delecolle,
Rob Cristofaro,
Tammy Brainard &
Tony Arcabascio**
When: **1999**
Where: **New York, USA**
Website: **www.alifenyc.com**

▶ (RAEKWON/WU-TANG CLAN)

Alife was born in 1999 when Arnaud Delecolle, Rob Cristofaro, Tammy Brainard and Tony Arcabascio joined together to open their first retail space in Orchard Street, New York. This outlet served as both their office and a shop, as well as an exhibition space, and laid the foundations of what has become one of today's most influential retail landscapes in downtown New York. Since then, Alife has gone from strength to strength, to become one of the most genre-defining and coveted independent streetwear labels. Its influence stretches far beyond the traditional approach of merely owning and running a brand, to include a footwear brand, RTFT by ALIFENYC, as well as a creative agency, ALIFECREATIVE.

Acting as an international retailer that also offers creative services, Alife has been able to help redefine streetwear from within: via ALIFECREATIVE, it has been responsible for producing such influential work such as the creative direction for *Mass Appeal* magazine, as well as developing art and retail installations with New York heavyweights, Deitch Projects and the Levi's and Alife Retail installation. Alife is one of the most directional and influential brands to have emerged out of the home of streetwear, New York, and will no doubt continue to play a major part in the international scene.

What has Alife come to mean in the marketplace as a whole?

I believe that we are a leader in the genre that we work within. We think Alife has played a vital part in creating the marketplace that you are referring to. The sneaker craze as we see it now was sparked by the introduction of the Alife Rivington Club in New York City. Research the time line of 'lifestyle' boutiques and sneaker shops and when they arrived on the scene. Alife's business plan has been mimicked across the globe as a working model. We have opened up new avenues for an audience that wasn't being marketed to in the past and created the opportunity for the big brands to sell speciality products, which are currently ruling the marketplace. We love what we do and we do it for the love.

Taking an idea through all the stages of fabrication to the point where it actually becomes a tangible product seems a mystery to most people. Alife has opened multiple stores over the years. Can you describe the process and how the Alife team gets it all done?

The projects that we involve ourselves in are usually projects that we believe are uplifting to the lifestyle we are engaged in. We come up with a plan that is tangible to execute with a defined final goal. We are hands-on from beginning to completion. One thing that we believe brings such great value to the Alife process is our ability to go in a different direction from what the market is currently offering.

What shops, spaces and locations is Alife deriving inspiration from when creating the look for its own spaces?

Our inspiration comes from all over. A lot of the time, it's timeless or classic. We stay away from the perceived trends of the moment. It is the type of space we believe our products would be most happy in.

Concerning customer reaction to a space, what is Alife's goal regarding consumer experience in the shops?

Our consumers are the people that are driving this market. They know what is going on all over the world in terms of this lifestyle. We like to give them the most that we can when entering one of our spaces:

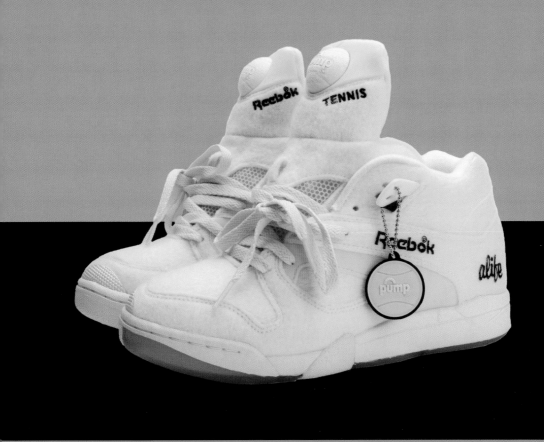

from the music to the quality of craftsmanship of the shop, to the quality of our product, to the shopping bag when they leave the space. It is all thought through at the building stage. We like to give our customers an experience that they will remember for one reason or another.

Where is Alife going as a brand?
The Alife brand is becoming much more focused on being an independent entity. By this I mean that we are trying to encompass all aspects of our business from manufacturing to distribution all in the way that we feel is most comfortable for ourselves. We are looking at the global picture and how our brand is going to get there. That process that is starting now. It is exciting and nervous as we begin this new level of Alife.

What does the new location in Vancouver offer Alife, and what led to the opening of this store?
Alife Vancouver offers the same as we offer our customers in NYC. The shop came to fruition because of the interest of former pro-skateboarder Tony Ferguson.

What does the future hold for the Alife team?
Constant movement, so keep your ears open. Ultimately the goal would be to once again take this marketplace somewhere that has yet to be evolved. Peace.

BOUNTY HUNTER

▶ One-off life-size toy in the Bounty Hunter store

Founded by: **Hikaru & Taka**
When: **1995**
Where: **Tokyo, Japan**
Website: **www.bounty-hunter.com**

ALL
OTHER
TOYS
SUCK

If Bounty Hunter could be expressed as a magic formula, it would be: US Toy + Punk Rock = Bounty Hunter. Hikaru and Taka, the brand's co-owners, both share a rebellious attitude, which brought them together as creative and commercial partners: they run on instinct, with a hatred of habit and repetition, and a deep desire to avoid following trends.

With Bounty Hunter, Hikaru and Taka have found a means of creatively expressing both their backgrounds and their deep knowledge of American youth culture – Hikaru from US toys, Taka from skateboarding – and in doing so have created one of the leading streetwear and urban toy brands. Hikaru's mother worked at a US

Navy base in Japan, and as a result, his early childhood was dominated by American toys and popular culture – it was something he simply grew up with. One of Hikaru's favourite toys was the 'Talking GI Joe', a rare item in Japan in those days, and even though he didn't understand what GI Joe was saying, it became (and remains) a personal favourite and a key reference to the toys Bounty Hunter creates.

Meanwhile, Taka was a high school student when the skateboarding boom hit Japan. He became fascinated not just with the art of skateboarding, but with the culture that went with it (not least because of its illegal and antisocial undertones). Taka brought years of acquired skateboarding manners

and attitude with him when he joined Hikaru to launch Bounty Hunter.

In May 1995, only six months after they decided to creatively and commercially join forces, they opened their first store. The original shop was some distance from the centre of Tokyo, and despite being ahead of the times when they launched, they've since become an established part of the streetwear scene in Japan. In fact, it would not be an exaggeration to say that Bounty Hunter played a major part in creating the urban toy boom we are now so familiar with.

When they first started out, there was no budget available for such luxuries as renting an office or warehouse space, and hiring assistants was simply out of the

question. While Hikaru was on a trip to source and buy stock for the store, Taka looked after the shop and vice versa. Their initial approach was a 'junk store' look – they carried a wide and eclectic range of goods such as collectible band t-shirts, comic books, toys (particularly *Star Wars* figures), sweets and their own t-shirt designs. Each stocked item meant something special and was carefully selected. Even the brand name represented their inspirations in popular culture and was taken from the name of the bounty hunter, Boba Fett, in the *Star Wars* films.

By 1997, business was thriving and their logo, designed by Hikaru and the 7STAR DESIGN team, had become easily recognizable in the streetwear scene and their logo-driven t-shirts were sold out as soon as they hit the shelves. Building on the success of the original Tokyo store, they opened others in Osaka, Nagoya, Fukuoka and Sendai.

Hikaru and Taka then did something which was unthinkable by many back in 1997, and in hindsight, it was a little crazy: they created, produced and released their own custom-made toy, Kid Hunter. Originally, Kid Hunter was a t-shirt artwork produced by the artist Skate Thing in the same style as an American cereal box character. When Hikaru and Taka saw the

sketches for the character, they knew it could be made into a toy and immediately went about making it happen. As soon as they saw the prototype of the Kid Hunter toy, they started thinking about creating more toys. Their second toy, released in 1997, combined cereal box characters and the image of a band Hikaru admired. The toy was called Skull Kun.

From those two early designs, Bounty Hunter have continued to come up with new, exciting and highly original toys. Just a few of the highlights since 1997 include The Great One – a toy influenced by ice hockey, released in 1997 – and the military-influenced Pagoda Kun from 1999 (Pagoda is the name of the Japanese Special Forces). In 2000–01, Wrag Chang, Hensley, Sameru Kun and a series of toy animals were created. In 2002, they released Mechagodzilla, closely followed by mechanical versions of Skull Kun, Sameru Kun, Mekaru Kun and Meka Sameru Kun. Each toy was greeted with much acclaim, but following the release of the 'Made in Japan' Skeru Kun and Catru Kun, Bounty Hunter called a halt to producing original toys.

Given the great success they were experiencing, their decision might sound strange, but as Bounty Hunter looked at the flood of toys

on the market, and the way in which toys had become very trendy, they found themselves in conflict with the core values of their brand – a rebellious attitude and a deliberate strategy of not following trends.

But in typical rebel style, once the boom slowed, they started up the production of toys again. In 2006, a pop candy-coloured Skull Kun was released, followed by a long-awaited new character, Moguru Kun, inspired by a mythical Japanese creature. Alongside the reintroduction of their own toys, Bounty Hunter have also forged working relationships with Disney and Marvel comics.

Bounty Hunter doesn't focus on market research or developing its toys and apparel in any given direction. Instead, it places emphasis on pure inspiration. Hikaru and Taka have never forgotten that Bounty Hunter is a toy store first and foremost, and that by holding firm to the experiences and culture that they are based in, they'll stay in the foreground of the streetwear scene.

With special thanks to Yass Endo

▶ View of the Bounty Hunter store

BRKN
HOME

Founded by: **Kenta Goto & Joshua Pong**
When: **2001**
Where: **Vancouver, Canada**
Website: **www.brknhome.com**

Brknhome (pronounced broken home) was established in Vancouver, home to some of streetwear's most prominent brands and designers. Although not immediately obvious as a streetwear destination, Vancouver has been known as the 'new' New York in insider circles for quite some time, with more and more high-end streetwear shops and brands setting up there. Brknhome was started, and is still run, by Kenta and Joshua, both of whom played a significant role in streetwear prior to setting up their own brand.

What does the term streetwear mean to you personally, as well as a designer?

Kenta: Street to me is where it all starts. From the ground up, street is the seed to all other fashion. I like to see streetwear brands lead the trend in fashion. Like back when heads were rocking the grunge look before Marc Jacobs did for Perry Ellis. To me, streetwear is the product of an evolution of different styles and fashion of punk, hip hop, and skate cultures. Some people feel the need to categorize and give a name to something so that they can better understand it. But streetwear is more easily defined by what it is not: it is not designed for the masses, and nor is it designed with a particular market in mind. It is not produced in great numbers to be sold at huge retail outlets and chain stores and is not to be defined by one look or style.

Joshua: Street can be anything. It's how someone chooses to wear an item. My favourite pieces are just common workwear. It's really about your lifestyle and not a brand that tells you 'this is street'.

How did you become involved in this subculture?

Kenta: the biggest influence was growing up in the skateboarding culture which allowed me to be open-minded about everything, but particularly in the arts. Skateboard graphics always intrigued me. I chose my decks by whatever graphics appealed to me first, then I chose the one with the shape I was most happy with. As a skater, the music I listened to were bands and artists that were featured on the skate videos I watched. At the start, most of the music was by smaller indy bands from California. Then as the skating evolved and became influenced by hip hop, so did my taste in music. But all the time, I was exposed to new music, and not what was playing on the radio at the time. With music always comes fashion. From pinned Dickies to size

◄ Lions t-shirt

▲ Butterfly t-shirt

40" Blind jeans, and Airwalk NTS to Puma suedes, we looked and dressed differently. Growing up, I saw that many of the fashion trends and details that we used to rock would start showing up on more mainstream artists and even on the catwalks, before being accepted into the mass market. Seeing this, I realized we were a part of the younger generation doing our own thing, but we had also been influencing others around us. I also saw that some of the more influential skaters were setting up their own brands, and artists creating the branding and visual identities for skate companies were setting up their own design firms.

Joshua: We've been following street culture since our high school days in the late 1980s to the 1990s. Everything from skate to hip hop. Personally I was obsessed with all things hip hop, from music to art, and above all, style and culture. Art and design was part of my public schooling and I was always into advertising, packaging, record and tape covers and logos. During the mid-1990s, I got involved with heads who were getting down with graffiti and bombing freight cars and doing legit work on canvases. I met a lot of artists like Loomit, Phil Frost and Barry McGee who I looked up to and drew inspiration from. Having this as an outlet was exciting and I spent a lot of time with like-minded dudes who were equally keen on all things street. Sneakers and clothing were always part of our lifestyle, be it Nike, adidas, tim boots or army gear, alongside Polo and Nautica and prep labels. Being so close to New York, Toronto got a good taste of the music, styles and slang of east coast America.

How do you see the development of streetwear, especially in terms of the advent of the internet?

Kenta: The advent of the internet has changed everything. Streetwear was once very limited, and only available through a few retailers in the big metropolitan cities around the world. Maybe you were lucky enough to have a cousin that lived in the big city and was into the same things and knew exactly where the shop was and what you wanted. In Toronto, we didn't always have access to the newest gear. We'd see fresh gear worn by a rapper on TV, or new sneakers on a skater in a magazine, but often they weren't attainable in Toronto. So we'd drive over two hours down to cross the border into Buffalo, NY just to buy gear and hunt down what you couldn't get back home. Now, anyone can go online and find a retailer to purchase these 'limited' items. Also, with the current trend in blogs, consumers are often told what's new and what the hot 'must-have items' are. The internet has too much information

▼ RoboSkull t-shirt

for consumers to handle, and creates confusion about what they actually like, and what they should like. It has taken away some of the mystique and the underground factor of streetwear. On the positive side, the internet has provided an opportunity for small brands to increase their business to virtually every corner of the world. And as designers, we can access information and references or find a retailer on the other side of the world with an impressive brand list and send them a catalogue. We see so many great collaborations between artists and brands now because it can be done so much easier and faster via the internet. It's hard to say where this is all going to take the market, but for brknhome, we've made a conscious decision to stay away from direct online sales and be selective about the retailers we do business with.

Joshua: With so much available at your fingertips as a consumer, dudes don't dig or research now like we did back in the day. People are quick to purchase whatever they see as hot from websites. I'm a consumer myself, especially when I travel. I mean there's a lot of good stuff coming out, and labels with really good ideas. But amongst all this good stuff is crap, followed by poor quality and bad taste. Brknhome has been a t-shirt company so far, so we are really careful about what we design and how we present our work, because how many t-shirt brands are out there? A crazy amount, and the market is flooded and it isn't all good. We make things we enjoy and just want like-minded heads to catch an idea and cop it if they like. It's not a mass-produced item and it's a sincere product we provide. I just want these guys to dig a little deeper and ask themselves why they want certain things. Is it because they saw it on the web, or is it because they really like a design? And were they even into this whole thing before the internet and magazines started catering to this market? Just go and educate yourself a little and the big picture becomes clearer.

How does your geographical position influence you in your work and your business?

Kenta: Based in Vancouver, we feel like we get a good perspective of the market. Being on the west coast, the lifestyle here has more

◀ American t-shirt

▲ Ashtray t-shirt

▲ Snake t-shirt

▲ Zebra t-shirt
▶ Unreleased brknhome design

parallels to Los Angeles than New York, but as the 'gateway to Orient' the city and its people are in touch with what's going on in Asia as well. A lot of our graphics are based on vices and things that may not be good for society, but these things make us human. Vancouver has a huge drug abuse problem in the lower east side. Although we have personal opinions regarding these issues, we try to present them without taking a stance for or against them. We just present it as a subject and people can take it any way they'd like. Canada is home to some of the best manufacturing facilities if you are looking for quality goods. Even though the costs of materials, printing and manufacturing are higher in Canada, we can stand behind the quality of our goods.

Joshua: It's a great place to look at the world from. Seeing what's bubbling here and there and then in turn, find ourselves able to put our own spin on things. Canada has a good sense of humour and the talent pool is impressive. So I still get inspired by my surroundings. But a good trip to New York or Europe doesn't hurt.

How are you commercially successful as well as being true to yourself and to the brknhome brand?
Being true to ourselves and to our brand is our number one priority. Commercial success isn't something we are too concerned with at the moment. We have stuck to our ideals and our concept of

the brand since day one. In the beginning we had a list of shops in America that we wanted to place our products in. We didn't want any compromises: we knew which shops we wanted to work with, so we didn't send any catalogues to other shops. We just kept trying until these shops took notice and took a chance on us. Now that we are pretty much in all of the shops from the original list and have great working relationships with all of them, we like to think that we have succeeded. Aside from keeping true to our brand we want to push new ideas and help to reinvent 'street' style and flavour. We are now trying to add to our lines of products and work with select shops and other like-minded artists.

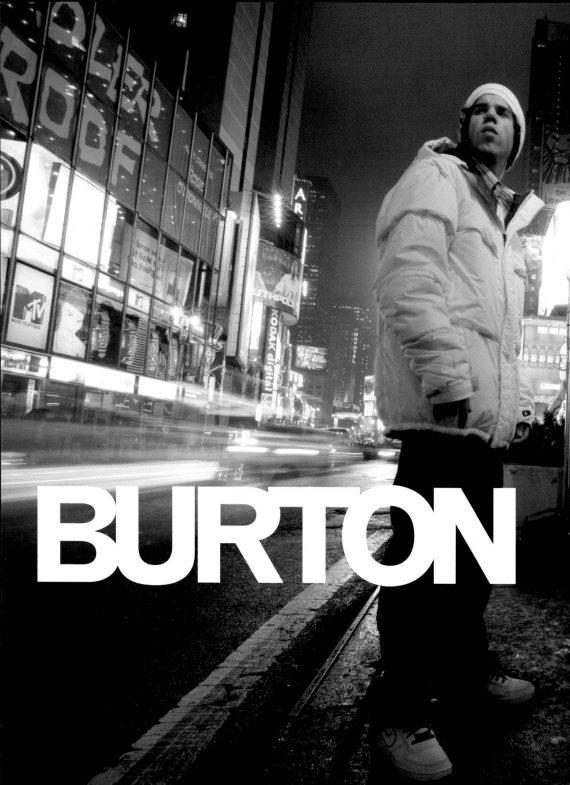

Founded by: **Jake Burton**
When: **1977**
Where: **Vermont, USA**
Website: **www.burton.com**

▲ Analog Foreman jacket
▼ Burton Element jacket and Seams beanie

▲ Analog Cryodown 2 jacket

The technical aspect of streetwear is important: the athletic nature of skateboarding and snowboarding requires a certain functionality and durability. Burton were the originators of such technical streetwear, and as Creative Director of Burton and its other brands (Gravis Footwear, Analog, Idiom and Red), Greg Dacyshyn has been responsible for some of the most influential designs and international prominence in this field.

What does the term streetwear mean to you, from a personal and a business point of view?

Streetwear has always been the antithesis of couture. Couture has the stigma of being luxury clothing lines created in big ivory towers in Europe. Streetwear, however, is inspired by and created at a street level. Streetwear to me has always implied smaller, grassroots or urban-based beginnings, with individuals involved in local downtown scenes, whether it be art, music, fashion, design or in our case, action sports (skating, snowboarding, surfing). Many of these core, urban-inspired brands become big apparel companies, but their roots are intact and that drives and defines them. I don't sense that couture comes from such a clear mandate, platform or identity, which I think is the critical link to having a successful streetwear brand.

How did you get involved in streetwear, and when?

I've always been a pop culture junkie and was always infatuated with sneaker culture as a little kid. Sneakers unto themselves were one of the purest representations of street culture early on. Clothing followed for me, of course, and

I was into the skate and surf brands when they first started to grow. Subsequently I got into Burton, when I discovered snowboarding. I am also obsessed with vintage brands and pop culture, like comics, personalities and sports heroes. Muhammad Ali and Bruce Lee are two of my all-time heroes. And I'll watch shows all day long about the 1970s, 1980s or 1990s. I love that every decade has a look and feel, a distinct music culture, a spirit and a handful of iconic brands. But to answer your question, I started designing and creating streetwear when I arrived at Burton Snowboards. I started in the product department, and eventually became the company's global Creative Director. Now I get to live the dream every day, by reaching into my mental arsenal of information and inspiration related to fashion, music, trends and history, to help direct and define our new product collections each season. At Burton we ensure that in addition to style and design, everything is innovative and has integrity. That goes for our streetwear too. Fashion meets function is the perfect marriage which many brands strive for, but few succeed at. At Burton, it's a given.

► Burton Just shirt, Wolf t-shirt and Ronin 3L jacket

▼ Analog Brian Sumner Jeans

Where do you think streetwear's strengths and weaknesses lie?

The coolest streetwear comes from the coolest and most talented individuals. Look at Stüssy, an action-sport pioneer in creating a viable global surf and skate lifestyle brand. That all came from Shawn Stüssy, who had a clear vision of the market from the start. Burton is similar. We are the global leaders in snowboarding: Jake Burton pioneered the sport, the industry, the infrastructure, everything, all because he had a vision and objective of bringing this sport to the world. Not because it was a quick trend or a fad. But because it was fun, challenging and soulful. In thirty years we've never lost track of that message and we make sure that everything we do helps to build snowboarding and continues to define its lifestyle. That goes for our streetwear too. If we don't stay pure to who we are and what our personality is, then our clothing and products mean nothing.

As for weaknesses, I worry about saturation. There are thousands of brands trying to jockey for the same spot. But only the pure and strong survive. You've got to have a reason and a vocation to make great products that endure. Consumers are more savvy than ever and they'll call you out in a minute if you don't deliver. So you have to work a thousand times harder than the next guy to rise above it.

Where is streetwear going?

Nowhere and everywhere. This takes me back to your first question of couture versus streetwear. After such a wide berth between the two sectors, this is rapidly shrinking. Chanel is streetwear; Louis Vuitton is streetwear. Models are taking up snowboarding and trying to emulate our lifestyle. High fashion and street fashion are now blended. The guys at DSquared do whatever the hell they want and suddenly it's a couture sweater that says 'fuck off' on the front. The irreverence of street is now demanded at the highest levels of fashion. And at street level, the quality and detailing of high fashion is a must-have. It's interesting and exciting to watch the two worlds merge: as the rules bend, brands like Burton can continue to push them to the next level.

What memorable events had an impact on you and the culture of streetwear?

Travelling and immersing myself in different cultures has had a huge influence on me. And meeting designers like Paul Smith, Hiroshi Fujiwara, Stash, riders like Trevor Andrew, Jeffy Anderson (R.I.P.), Keir Dillon, Jake Burton and the Burton team. People like this inspire you to grow and be better at what you do.

The key to success in any business is longevity. How do you apply this to your design work and business practice?

As I discussed earlier, it is all about longevity. You don't want to be so niche that you close yourself off. In denim, the prices keep rising,

but it must suck for brands to only have their one week of fame in *US* magazine, before another one is 'hot'. How do you specialize and diversify at the same time? You establish a bullet-proof product platform, and push yourself to make the lines better every season. At Burton, we make the most technical, industry-leading products, as well as creating cool and stylish products to appeal to a wider audience than just the consumer on the mountain. With that challenge comes the opportunity to pioneer, which is what we've done. Snowboarding is surrounded by a lifestyle and we wanted to express that in a range of products that can be worn year-round and off the hill.

That was a big move for us, but we waited until we felt we knew what we wanted to do, and what the market was missing. You need to constantly be aware of where your market is going, and what you need to do to stay ahead. Don't be afraid to let go of products that are done, and fight for those you need forever. Lastly, working alongside key taste-makers and in our case, the best snow-boarders in the world,

is an absolute. You cannot claim to make the best or most stylish products if the best and most stylish individuals don't back that up.

What do you love about this culture?

Everything. Myself, my wife and my close friends are all part of a global community, and it is a gift and privilege to have that. It's never dull, never the same and you can be true to who you are. We spend time in New York, LA, Tokyo, Hong Kong and Europe. And that is what feeds our energy and creativity. I cannot imagine doing anything else, and I hope that in some way, I leave a legacy as a result.

◄ Element jacket, foreshadow hoodie and seams beanie
▼ Canal jacket and maize polo shirt
▲▲ Analog squad and spitfire hoodies

COMMON

WEALTH

Founded by: **Omar Quiambao**
When: **2004**
Where: **Virginia, USA**
Website: **www.cmonwealth.com**

Commonwealth is a 900-square-foot retail space in the growing area of Ghent in downtown Norfolk, Virginia. Known for its diverse culture and neighbourhoods, Norfolk encompasses a community with deep roots in surfing, skateboarding, sports and hip hop. Sports stars such as Allen Iverson, Alonzo Mourning and Michael Vick, as well as musicians like the Neptunes, the Clipse, Kenna, Famlay, Missy Elliott and Timbaland all live there. Not to mention those veteran skateboard pros, including Andy Howell, Sergie Ventura and Kyle Berard. Commonwealth aims to fulfil

the demand for street/fashion/athletic brands. It carries lines that reflect the new creative and independent spirit in the world of streetwear and works with recognized artists, designers and photographers.

What does the term streetwear mean to you, from a personal and a business perspective?

Streetwear has always been an extension of skateboarding. It always had this intangible connection with the creative perspective a skateboarder has when he views everyday objects in an architectural terrain. It's different from the average person – we tend to see these objects and places with a different function in mind. That kind of viewpoint coupled with the inherent DIY attitudes

applied to the fields of art, design, photography, fashion, music and film has helped develop what I consider to be street culture today.

As for the business view, I guess streetwear is the translation of this lifestyle into packaged goods that are sold. For some, the products can be trite and really suck the soul out of what people believe in. But the profits of consumerism can become a necessary evil to be able to support one's life and pay the bills.

How did you get involved in streetwear and when?

I first dropped in on my cousin's halfpipe in 1983. All the while, the majority of my youth I was involved in art schools/classes. It started more with just classical drawing,

HONOR
AMONGST
THIEVES

CROOKS
and Castles

for THE
GREATER
GOOD

Commonwealth·

FOURSQUARE

Akademiks Aptitude Test

TERRORIST
PATRIOT
ACTIVIST
SCAPEGOAT
POLITICIAN

Graphics by Omar Quiambao

...hen, as I got into high school, trade school and college (Pratt Institute), it transformed into advertising and design. Then a few years after moving to California to work for different skate and snow brands, it became product development and brand building/management. Over the last decade I've been fortunate enough to use my talents for some of the better and more influential brands in youth culture, skate, snow, urban or sportswear. I've worked for, or have done projects with, DC Shoes, Droors Denim, A# Alphanumeric, Special Blend, Foursquare, Zoo York, Akademiks, Mecca, And 1, and Converse.

I now involve myself in the business side of the culture, from being a consumer, launching a new menswear label, Rip-off & Duplicate/R&D and opening retail stores (Commonwealth). I also continue to work on projects with 10.Deep, Crooks & Castles, Stüssy, Reebok/Rbk, Creative Recreation and New Era.

Where do streetwear's strengths and weaknesses lie?

A main strength is that even though it is still fashion, it's deeper than just the clothes. The networking of talented people is extremely inspiring. Inspiring enough to influence the high and low brow in many scenes and cultures. The better brands or product come from understanding the people involved in this culture.

A weakness is that it started as an artistic or social movement but has lost meaning and started to shift focus entirely on to product and consumerism. It's not as easy to spot 'posers' or 'wannabes' these days as it was in the past. It would be a shame to think that a person can be easily accepted into a social group just by having the right brands. Nowadays kids can buy it off the internet. Whereas before you would have to travel to get certain brands or products. And th experience of taking that journey t get them is what gave the culture integrity, not the item itself.

Where is streetwear going?

The consumer by-products of this culture are really hitting the

▲ Graphics by Omar Quiambao

mainstream, through popular music, entertainment or the internet. As any counter culture becomes mainstream, it loses perspective. There will be the companies that choose to 'sell out' and water down what it is they do for the lowest common denominator. And there will be other companies that will be maintained through longevity. I believe those who should profit should have been truest to the culture and to themselves.

Which memorable events had an impact on you and also on street culture?
From the onset of stepping on to a skateboard, to hearing rap music for the first time. Most memorable for me are more personal rather than momentous events for the culture. Many of them are based on the people I've had the opportunity to work with. Also, being able to travel around the world and experience first-hand the lives of others. Ultimately that has been the strength and bond of this international culture.

The key to success in business is longevity. How do you apply this to your design work and business development?
When it comes to longevity, I believe the slow and steady win the race. In design, I believe in 'quality over quantity'. In business development there are many factors that have to be considered that you don't always have control over.

But in business practice, applying the golden rule of treating others how you want to be treated, including your employees, partners, co-workers, clients or customers seems to work pretty well.

What do you love about streetwear?
Meeting new people, exchanging ideas and learning new perspectives.

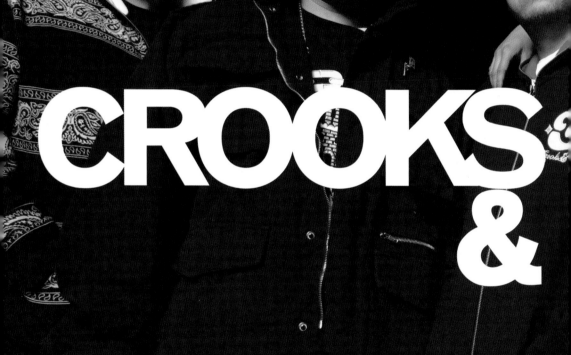

CROOKS &

CASTLES

Founded by: **Dennis Calvero**
When: **2002**
Where: **Los Angeles, USA**
Website: **www.crooksncastles.com**

▲ Above left to right: Fall/Winter 2006 collection

What does streetwear mean to you, from a personal and a business point of view?

From a personal point of view, streetwear is a class of fashion influenced by youth culture, street persona and action sports. From a business perspective, being classified as a streetwear brand allows you to market yourself to more than one type of customer.

How did you get involved in this culture, and when?

In the early 1990s, brands were poppin' up like Freshjive, bronze age, of course Stüssy, and were doing some different shit. I was doing an internship at Motown Records in the Miracle Mile District of Los Angeles. This was in 1994 or 1995. During one of my breaks, I stumbled across Union on La Brea. It was a new type of shop to me. The decor and the products it carried were different. Arnold Espiritu from GreyOne was working there at the time and we knew each other from back in the Gang Bang era. He blessed me with a Union shirt and I think I bought a backpack, or some shit. But after that experience I knew I didn't want to design CDs anymore.

Where do you think streetwear's strengths and weaknesses lie?

The main strength is streetwear's wide and creative diversity. Each brand seems to have its own identity, themes and style. An abundance of new streetwear lines could be a weakness, but we'll see who's still around in a few years.

Where do you think streetwear is going?

I see it going more mainstream. Streetwear is the new Urban!

Where do you want to take Crooks & Castles?

I'd like to take it to a level where it becomes a well-respected global brand, offering more than just apparel. A lifestyle brand. I mean I'm really counting on it to be my retirement plan!

Can you describe some of the more memorable events that had an impact on you, and on street culture?

Living in the East had a huge impact on me. I grew up in Los Angeles and experienced street culture during the late 1980s and 1990s. When there were dance crews back in the day like boogie unit, the daisy unit, system that dissed'em, hip hop hippies … all these dudes would have some kind of individual style. Street fashion was yet to come, but kids were rocking Polo, Gap, Nautica and would make it street.

The key to success in streetwear is longevity. How do you see this and how do you apply it to your design work and business development/practice?

Longevity is key especially if you wanna be around in a few years. I try to offer well-crafted products that can be in your closet for longer than a minute. I'm always trying to push our factories to produce high quality goods. Having a strong business plan provides you with what you will need and what you have to do to maintain steady growth. I'm more creative but am training myself to be more business-minded. It's tough sometimes, but with practice comes perfection.

What do you love about streetwear?

The possibility that something which started out as an idea will become a global identity.

CROWN

Crownfarmer is a creative outlet and clothing label founded by Bob Kronbauer that was initially set up to include three online zines before Kronbauer decided to make t-shirts instead. Crownfarmer's 'fourteen' project was its first foray into the realm of limited-edition t-shirts and included a range of fourteen designs created by a selected group of friendly artists, including Matt Irving from the Delphi Collective. After the success of that project, Crownfarmer went on to create regular seasons with t-shirts, scarves, jackets and bags, all designed by Kronbauer. At the same time, Kronbauer continued to bring together artists for special projects such as the coupled Crownfarmers series. 2006 will see big changes in the company, including a return to publishing with the release of the first book, *Little Giants*, which will showcase the work of an artist selected in an online ballot.

FARMER

Founded by: **Bob Kronbauer**
When: **2000**
Where: **Vancouver, Canada**
Website: **www.crownfarmer.com**

◀▲ 2004–06 t-shirt collection

When and how did you first become aware of streetwear as a subculture?

I guess I wasn't aware that it actually WAS a subculture until a very long time after I became involved in it. I first started skateboarding in high school, and have always been interested in art direction and clothing design too, so I guess I kinda naturally fell into it.

What were the defining moments in terms of this subculture for you?

That's a tough question. Do you remember when Freshjive went from just being weird raver gear that skateboarders made fun of, into something cool and sought-after by the coolest of the cool kids? There's probably a defining moment in there somewhere but I don't know exactly when it happened, or exactly how it happened I guess. I think it has helped a lot with the marketing of smaller companies, like ours for example. Lots of people would never have heard of us if it weren't for news scrolls and bloggers who found us and wrote about what we're doing, and then linked to our site. It's also good for inspiration, learning about other brands online, but the main downfall that I've seen is that with everybody looking at the same internet, a lot of stuff starts to look the same. So in the end, I prefer to find inspiration for the line elsewhere.

At what stage in your life did streetwear become more than just a hobby to you, and why?

Have you ever worked at a gas station while shooting photos for skate magazines in your spare time? Have you ever constructed jeans from scratch on the side, just for fun, whilst also delivering pizzas for a living? When I was about twenty I decided that I didn't want to work shit jobs anymore.

Dave Ortiz is one of New York's icons. He was raised there when skateboarding was still an underground sport rather than a product placement haven for large corporations, and formed part of a group who put skateboarding on the map. After working at Zoo York, before it was sold to the Ecko Empire, Dave left to set up his own brand and outlet – Dave's Quality Meat. Dave runs this fiercely independent brand with Chris Keefe. Dave talks here about what streetwear means to him and how he first got involved.

I guess while I was working at Zoo York and hanging out at Supreme with Chris in the mid-1990s, we were around the best guys, like the Stashs, the Futuras the Rodneys from Zoo, the Eli Gesners from Zoo and the Adams. Chris was around the Surrs, the Joes and the Annas.

It's funny what you can learn from your surroundings: some things could be good, some things could be bad. You have to take what you learn and apply it. That is what Chris and I did: we learned and didn't burn any bridges. We play an honest game, a fair game, without trying to hurt anyone – 'just helping others' is our motto. This City we live in reminds me of an impressionist painting – layer upon layer of stuff – this place is dirty, loud, beautiful, harsh, loving, dangerous, fun, changing and it's real but it takes many parts to make it the most interesting place on earth. You can see everything if you really look around. I always see something new that I've never seen before I love that about NYC, I can't imagine being from some place else, but who's to say this is the jelly and the jam? I'm sure I'd feel the same way if I was from

Founded by: **Dave Ortiz & John & Chris Keefe** When: **2004** Where: **New York, USA** Website: **www.davesqualitymeat.com**

London. I think every place on earth has a certain thing that makes a person who's from there feel special. I guess you could call that 'Home Syndrome'. There are places that one aspires to go. What I'm getting at is that you can make it anywhere, whatever makes your heart feel good. So never be bummed about where it is you're from: one day you will get to see the other parts of this great world we live in and appreciate it for what it is – a painting of life.

What is streetwear to you? Is it something that people use to stand out from the crowd?

I see a lot of it coming from NYC. It's everywhere, from the kids that go to school and have to wear a uniform. They all dress the same but the way the go about it is different. Walk past Tompkins Square Park and you see other ways of streetwear: the punk damage kids with pins in their faces and tattoos and tight-ass pants and chain wallets. The gay guy and his dog with matching jackets? It's everything around us that makes streetwear. When I think of myself and streetwear, I'm that nerd guy who doesn't really care what people think of what I'm wearing. It doesn't change who I am as a person. You can ask my girl – she thinks

▲▼▶ The DQM shop, New York

▲ ▲ ▲ The DQM shop, New York

I dress like an idiot. She calls me Zoo Bum coz I still have jeans that are ten years old that I got from Zoo York, and she's always hounding me to dress better. What am I to do – go out and get a blazer jacket and wear a hoody under my jacket? NO! I can't pull that off – it's not me. Or should I have the dopest sneakers on that just came out and no one has, then go ahead and skate in them and ruin them? Sometimes I think of it like Einstein. I wish I had one suit for everyday of the week that looked the same. Then I could use the time I was wasting on choosing what to wear for better things like painting or being an uncle to my niece or being a better boyfriend – there is always room for that one. Again, it's back to what I believe in – one should do what one feels like.

DELPHI

Founded by: **Matt Irving**   When: **2003**   Where: **San Francisco, USA**   Website: **www.delphicollective.com**

▲ Stereo Skateboard decks by Matt Irving

▲ Delphi Collective t-shirts

A Canadian living in California, Matt Irving has created some of the most notable skateboard designs in recent years and has extended the influence of the skate scene into youth culture around the world. Irving first worked for the legendary skateboard company Stereo Skateboards – with Chris Pastras and the now-famous Hollywood actor Jason Lee – where he was responsible for the majority of artistic output, whilst also designing for Nike Skateboarding and Element Skateboards. He is now part of the Elementrio Art Team at Element Skateboards with Todd Francis and Don Pendleton. The Delphi Collective is a multi-faceted agency that creates mind-blowing designs and a unique clothing line.

What does the term streetwear mean to you, from a personal and business point of view?
To me, streetwear sums up a very particular subculture that sprouted up across the globe through like-minded people who wanted to create clothing, books and collectibles. Since it's become a worldwide epidemic and everyone has their personal take on the word, it's hard to have one term to sum it all up. Outsiders instantly default to graffiti and hip hop as the defining

factors of streetwear, but it goes so much deeper than that, depending on the background of the people who are doing the work. If you have roots in graffiti or hip hop, then you would naturally gravitate to that type of subject matter. But there's plenty of streetwear brands that aren't doing that. Personally, I gravitate towards skateboarding because it was my entire youth and continues to run my life today. Half the fun with skating is pushing around in the city with your friends, going on road trips and stuff like that. When I could afford a brand new board, I would hold out for one that was the right size but it had to have a graphic that I was really hyped on. I don't want to spend my hard-earned money on stuff that I'm not backing one hundred per cent. I'd way rather hold out and spend more money on something I love, than less money on something that's mediocre. I feel like this sort of relates to the streetwear world because most of the people making the stuff are picky as hell, just like me. It's obvious when someone's put the energy into designing something that is legit.

How did you get involved in streetwear, and when?
Skating made me start to realize there was a subculture that existed

without advertising and mainstream exposure. It was the little companies that didn't necessarily have the most popular team riders but maintained a certain degree of purity with how they skate that no one can deny. Usually, they also had a unique approach to graphics and art, which helped solidify the company as a whole. Zoo York, Stereo, Girl, Chocolate, Mad Circle, Silverstar and Blueprint were the subversive companies that I was into in the 1990s. Supreme was probably the turning point when I started to realize that a world existed beyond skating. Seeing the occasional issue of *Lodown* also opened up my eyes.

Where do streetwear's strengths and weaknesses lie?
One of the most obvious strengths is people's blind faith in what they do. A lot of people involved with streetwear are just trudging away in the trenches doing whatever happens to feel right to them. These are the true innovators who become leaders with time because of their conviction. However, the weaknesses of streetwear come from this too. As popularity grows, more and more people want to get involved and everyone copies each other until it becomes a

homogenous cesspool. The best things always start out innocent and slowly become bastardized. Maybe this is too pragmatic an outlook, but I've seen it happen with skateboarding, and it's hard for the little guy to succeed once pop culture has decided to jump in. I'm not talking specifically about corporate involvement – I actually think that can be good if it's with sincere reasoning – I'm more concerned about the people and companies latching on to something that they see developing but that they don't understand. Skateboard magazines with bubble gum, deodorant and army recruitment ads are damaging to skating because they have no loyalty to the community and will pull out in a split-second. I could see that happening soon enough. What's to say that Monsieur Andre isn't going to be asked to be a guest on *Celebrity Jeopardy*?

Where do you think streetwear is going?

It'll go wherever it wants to go, so who knows? My gut instinct is that it'll maintain a level of originality for a number of years and then slowly be infiltrated by outsiders who have had their attention sparked in this direction because of the freshness and the untapped opportunity. It's up to the people who are creating streetwear to dictate where it goes and that is based on what is authentic to them at the time.

Where do you want to take Delphi?

The goal with Delphi is to maintain a level of quality, originality and innovation that doesn't follow the masses. To be able to co-op with people and companies on projects and exhibitions that we are proud of, keeping creativity in the forefront. I never want to make Delphi products that I don't like. I always want to keep the environmental impact in mind and try to offer alternative solutions to the companies that we work with.

What were the most memorable events that had an impact on you, and on streetwear?

Specific events are hard to isolate because it's such a fragmented community that doesn't have a dominant public forum or media to set the pace. Instead, it's hundreds of online forums and a wide array of magazines that are drastically different from each other. I find that I look to certain people and companies that I find intriguing. I really like what Hiroshi Fujiwara is doing because he is so focused on quality. I've been a fan of Silas for a very long time because of their simplicity. Stüssy has done an amazing job at staying focused on what they are about and they've set a bar that everyone else aspires to achieve. Visvim is up to some great stuff. *Made* magazine and *Arkitip* have done a great job at bringing in fresh perspectives and not following trends for the sake of it.

The key to success is longevity. How do you see this in relation to your design work and business development?

Shit, I don't know. Let's see if longevity can be attained and talk about it in ten years or so. I think that everyone is relatively new to this. I mean nobody has retired from it yet, right?

What do you love about streetwear?

I love that most people involved in it are self-motivated and have a burning desire to create stuff that strays from the average. It's not about making money: that's easy if you don't have any standards to adhere to. It's more about getting your ideas out to the masses and feeling proud of what you've created and believing in it absolutely one hundred per cent.

▲ Nike SB Dunk 'the hunter', 2004 and Delphi Collective Hat, 2006
▼ ▼ ▼ A selection of Delphi Collective designs

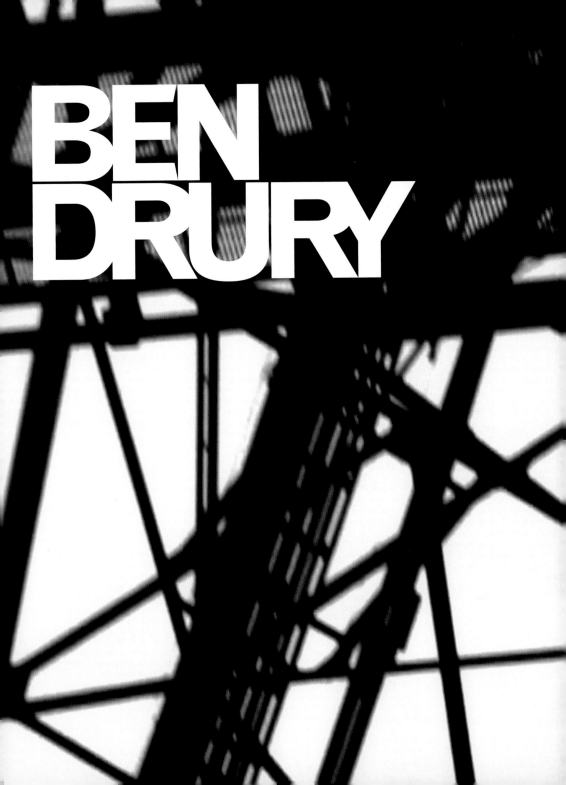

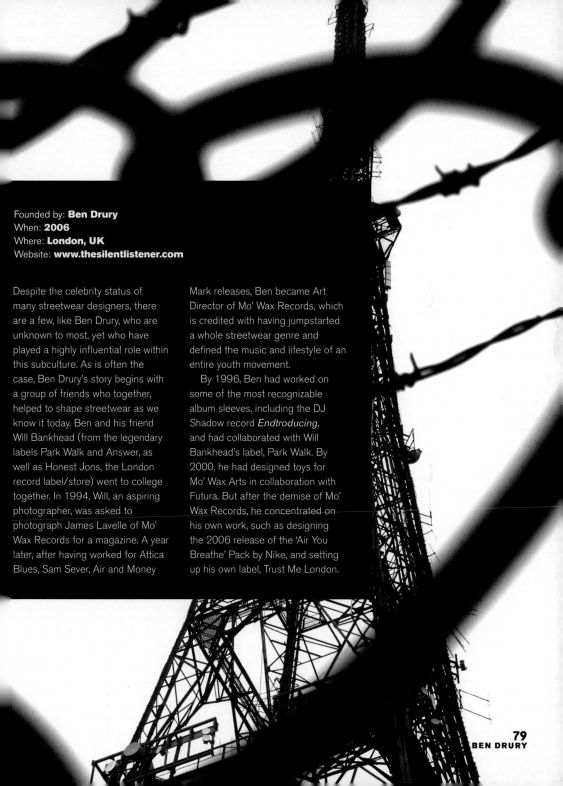

Founded by: **Ben Drury**
When: **2006**
Where: **London, UK**
Website: **www.thesilentlistener.com**

Despite the celebrity status of many streetwear designers, there are a few, like Ben Drury, who are unknown to most, yet who have played a highly influential role within this subculture. As is often the case, Ben Drury's story begins with a group of friends who together, helped to shape streetwear as we know it today. Ben and his friend Will Bankhead (from the legendary labels Park Walk and Answer, as well as Honest Jons, the London record label/store) went to college together. In 1994, Will, an aspiring photographer, was asked to photograph James Lavelle of Mo' Wax Records for a magazine. A year later, after having worked for Attica Blues, Sam Sever, Air and Money

Mark releases, Ben became Art Director of Mo' Wax Records, which is credited with having jumpstarted a whole streetwear genre and defined the music and lifestyle of an entire youth movement.

By 1996, Ben had worked on some of the most recognizable album sleeves, including the DJ Shadow record *Endtroducing*, and had collaborated with Will Bankhead's label, Park Walk. By 2000, he had designed toys for Mo' Wax Arts in collaboration with Futura. But after the demise of Mo' Wax Records, he concentrated on his own work, such as designing the 2006 release of the 'Air You Breathe' Pack by Nike, and setting up his own label, Trust Me London.

Streetwear is a relatively new term for something that most people either don't, or can't, define. Yet there is a collective understanding about what it is, and especially about what it is not. How do you define streetwear?

I find the addition of the word 'street' to anything, whether it be clothing, art or music, slightly demeaning. Any practitioner must surely aspire to create great clothing or art, or whatever else they're engaged in, rather than trying to cater for a specific, manufactured market aligned to a scene. No matter how wide-reaching it may be. There's a perception that 'streetwear' is a global phenomenon, but like everything else, when it's given a name, what was once alluring is lost.

When did you realize that you were involved in something special and new?

I've always been too busy to give this matter any thought.

Where do streetwear's strengths and weaknesses lie?

At its best, cool t-shirts. At its worst, crap t-shirts.

Which events had an impact on you, especially those that then had an impact on streetwear?

Personally speaking, I would say primarily meeting Will Bankhead at college in 1991. Not in itself a cataclysmic event but in the grand scale of things…. We plotted a course back then that (independently) we're pretty much still following today, not sure if that's a good or bad thing though.

Where do you think streetwear is going?

Nowhere.

In recent years, focus has shifted on to the product itself, rather than on incorporating the many elements of the streetwear subculture (such as skateboarding, music etc). How do you explain that and what do you think of that development?

Streetwear as a self-referential subculture holds no interest for me. Authenticity has to be fought for and its scars worn with pride.

▲ T-shirt graphics from Trust Me London

DUSTY

Founded by: **Paul Ma** When: **1996** Where: **Hong Kong, China** Website: **www.dusty.com.hk**

Hong Kong is the rising star in today's streetwear scene. The market in Hong Kong is by far one of the most lucrative in the world, and all aspects of streetwear culture have taken a firm hold there. The home-grown streetwear scene has been growing steadily over recent years and almost certainly predates the advent of the internet. Paul Ma set up Dusty, his own clothing line, over ten years ago in Hong Kong and now owns several shops and clothing lines. He has also worked on countless collaborations with some of the most respected artists worldwide. Paul has never forgotten why he started, and where, and promotes the streetwear scene in Hong Kong by supporting fresh young talent.

What is Dusty?

We are a clothing company based in Hong Kong and we started in 1996. We opened our first small store at the same time as setting up our company 'Hardcore' and we started with more skate-oriented clothing, especially since there really weren't any streetwear brands in Hong Kong at the time. A year later, my partner Max and I decided to start our own brand which we called Dusty. We both already had a good knowledge of production and sales so it seemed like a natural thing to do. At first we produced some simple cut-and-sew products since we didn't just want to be a t-shirt company. Now we have a full line which includes everything from accessories,

t-shirts, sweatshirts, bottoms as well as more complicated cut-and-sew products.

How did you get involved in streetwear?

When Max and I were still in Junior High School in the early 1990s we went clubbing quite often, and in those days were first exposed I guess. It was that mix between hip hop, rap, new age, house, punk and rock, the combination between skateboarding and music which really amazed us. Later on I became much more involved in all the different facets of this subculture.

What made you start your own clothing line?

▲ Spring/Summer Collection, 2007

Oh loads! I have always enjoyed the process of making clothing, sourcing, drawing, sampling and production: especially if I learned something new along the way. There are many aspects to making a line, from the above-mentioned elements, to washing, dyeing, sewing, printing, embroidering, packing and so on.

Which brands and designers influenced you?

Loads of other brands and designers, especially when I was younger. We looked at how other brands had set up their strategies, design concepts and management, then took all the good points from what we had seen, mixed them up and tried to apply them to Dusty.

What are the main differences between the scene in Hong Kong compared to New York, Tokyo or London?

Some people say the scene in Hong Kong is a bit slow, which it is not. I have travelled to Singapore, Taiwan, Japan, Korea, London and New York and quite honestly the scenes in all those places are all quite similar. The thing about Hong Kong though, is that most people and brands really only concentrate on their work here and don't do too much PR, so to the outside it looks as if we're not doing something, but it's quite the contrary.

How was 2006, your tenth year?

You know, 2006 was intense for us, as it was our ten-year anniversary.

Especially the last six months, we had all kinds of crazy projects and collaborations for the anniversary. First we did a photo exhibition with David Corio from New York. We then launched the 'Dusty City' compilation CD together with Love Da Records out here. We then released a series of t-shirts, called our 'Global Artist Series', which six different artists contributed to, including Kohei from Motive in Japan, Alyasha from Fibreops, Emmet and Will from Answer in London, Eric So from Hong Kong, Jeff Staple from New York and SIG from Redrum. We are all fans of those guys so it was more of an appreciation exercise for us. We also will release a Dusty/Be@rbrick but that's secret for now.

▼ Dusty x Medicom Be@rbrick collaboration

Dusty

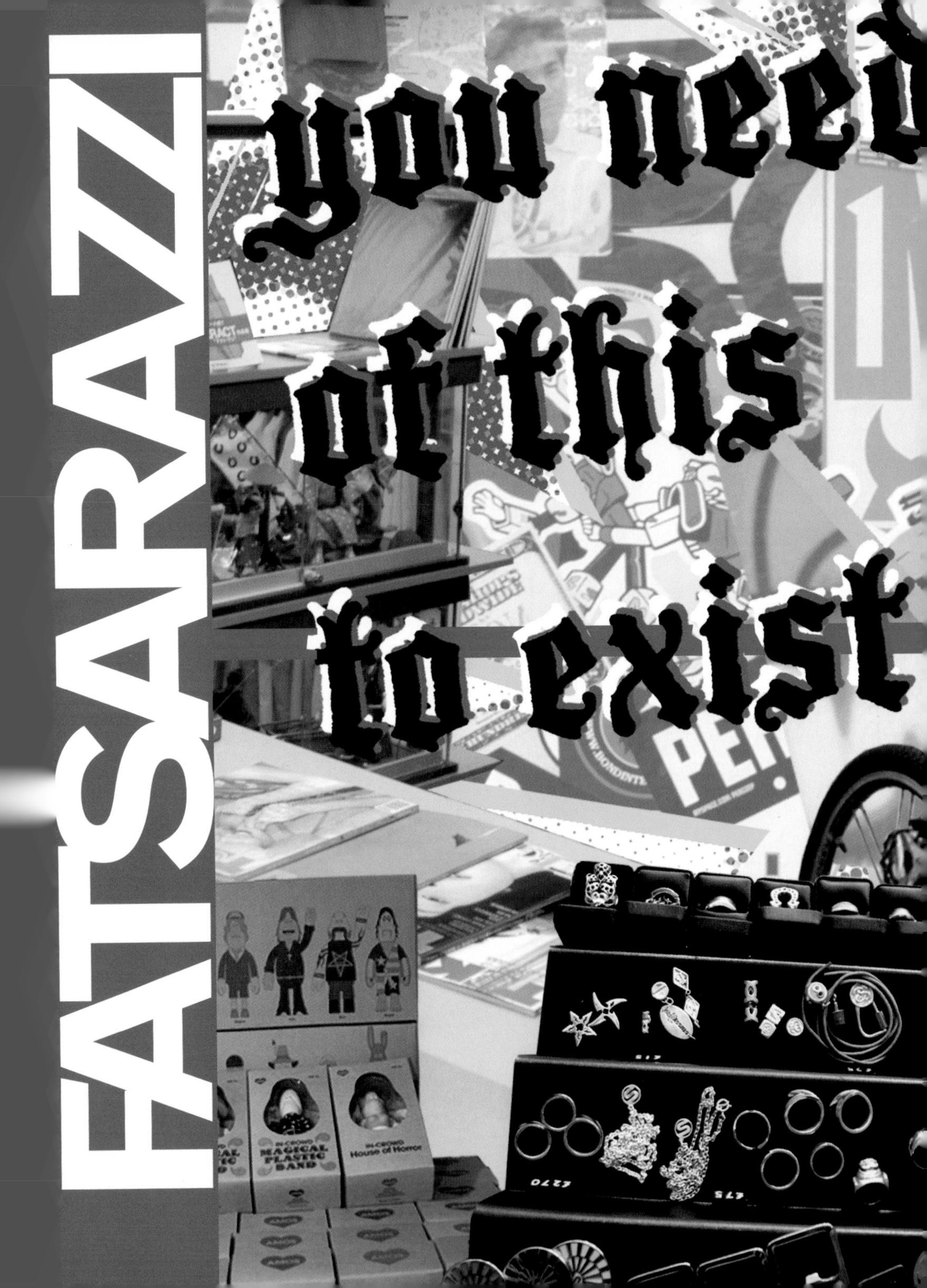

FATSARAZI

you need of this to exist

some

Founded by: **Fats Shariff**
When: **1980s**
Where: **London, UK**
Website: **www.fatsarazzi.co.uk**

Fats Shariff and his alter-ego, Fatsarazzi, define streetwear. Once part of the most integral European streetwear company, Gimme5, Fats is now *the* photographer for quality, insight and original streetwear treatments. He has worked on influential labels such as Gimme5, GoodEnough UK, A Bathing Ape, Silas, Vans and Maharishi, and also runs his own label/store, A Factor of Three. Fats offers a few thoughts on streetwear, in an essay entitled 'A Natural Progression'.

What I have come to like about streetwear and street culture is where, in my humble perception, the so-called ORIGINATORS have evolved to.

Having been openly involved with some of the good, the bad and some downright uglies of the profession over the last twenty years, I have seen a few things. For me, the birth of streetwear clothing came from a need for comfort, durability and expression. A small group of individuals willing to look out of the box saw an integral culture screaming to express themselves, bam! The rebirth of the t-shirt as new mass media.

Birth can be that simple, One becomes ten. Ten become one hundred. One hundred become a thousand and so on. With numbers comes cash, with cash comes expansion. The expansion moved to utility items that everyone wore

and if you look carefully, we still are. But rather than buy, let's make and put the pocket for your wrench right there, so when you fall it won't hurt.

Pockets moved and panels changed to make them work better. This even lead to the catwalk, where they have taken design classics and edited them to suit the times.

Back to the street. Items grew, sales grew, competition grew, the ORIGINATORS were growing, and machines needed feeding. One day they wake up and have a global presence and a global following. And, every day the competition grows. It is no easy task and I respect all who have achieved such heights and continue to do so. With the growth of labels and the growth

of the ORIGINATORS comes change. As for growth, I mean not only in a financial sense, but in sophistication and appreciation. Time progressed and the question became 'how to find that inspiration'.

As their appreciation grew, so did the field of vision, and this lead to the ORIGINATORS stepping further afield. Further afield meant Japan.

In 1985–95 all eyes were on how the many subcultures of style in Japan crossed so many boundaries. Japanese ORIGINATORS embody style and have a chameleon-like way of adapting in a progressive and inspiring manner. But Japan was hungry for this culture, and was eating it up. It read the recipe and added enhancing flavours.

Suddenly toys, watches, bags, furniture and a trend for 'double labels' emerged. By 1995, competition could not exist unless products went beyond what they were originally known for. The financial gains over the years made this possible. Clothing became a launch pad. Evolution or another subculture? A new crew emerged. Wiser, sharper, they had watched and learned. Technology allowed them to see things in a different way and the new ORIGINATORS were born. They began with the whole package, no build-up, no launch pad. And so it has continued, and will continue to progress and evolve into a new and improved culture of our time. Long may it continue!!!

FEIT

Founded by: **Tull Price & Rodney Adler**

When: **2001**

Where: **London, UK**

Website: **www.joinfeit.com**

◄ The Feit store, Australia

Sneakers are as much a part of the streetwear industry as t-shirts. The footwear market, however, is dominated by major brands, owing to pricing, production and pure marketing ability. But despite the odds, there are a few small independent footwear companies in the streetwear industry that have taken it upon themselves not to fight against the majors, but to carve a niche in which they can express their own individual creativity and knowledge. Feit is one such independent footwear brand. Thanks to incredible attention to detail and an uncompromising attitude in terms of design and exposure, Feit has

quickly gained a loyal worldwide following in the streetwear scene.

What does the term streetwear mean to you, from a personal and business point of view?
Personally, for me, streetwear is really nothing more than a descriptive word used to describe a type of clothing I have bought or worn

for a while. From a business point of view, it is a term used to try describing a certain style of clothes to people who don't really get or understand it from what they see.

How did you get involved in the streetwear culture, and when?

For me, it came from growing up listening to hip hop music and rolling around the streets. As a young teenager, finding some pieces which I guess would fit into the word 'streetwear' or the look of 'streetwear' was a great relief. If you weren't into sports only, skating only, surfing only or fashion only, you needed something else.

Where do streetwear's strengths and weaknesses lie?

Streetwear's strengths lie in its substantial roots. Streetwear is born from numerous influences, with few limits. Its weaknesses would be the same.

Where do you think streetwear is going?

Streetwear seems to be attracting more and more creative people, so I'm sure that as time progresses, these minds will continue to find innovative ways of pushing it, and art, forward. Streetwear seems to be growing up with the people who are into it.

What were some of the most memorable events that had an impact on you, and on streetwear?

I think some of the key events for streetwear occurred, for example, when people in prison wore their pants low (due to having no belts); when the Carhartt label was adopted into the hip hop era (with XL/ Beastie Boys giving it some pop and flavour); when Stüssy moved from surfwear; Eric haze, Futura, stash; and NY/LA, and Japan for fine-tuning what America started.

The key to success in streetwear (as in any other business) is longevity. How do you see this, and how do you apply it to your design work and business development/ business practice?

Design-wise, it's about creating things forever. Not just for now. For now, for the past and the future. Try as best as possible to take things slowly and one step at a time, which is hard – money sometimes makes it tough, but all you can do is try to keep fighting.

What do you love about this streetwear culture?

I love streetwear's creative edge and its ability to remain pure.

Founded by: **Jason Dill & Mike Piscitelli**
When: **2001**
Where: **New York & Los Angeles, USA**
Website: **www.fuckingawesome.net**

Jason Dill and Mike Piscitelli are the founders of Fucking Awesome. But Jason is better known as the unpredictable but amazing pro-skateboarder on Alien Workshop and DVS, while Mike is renowned for his incredible art and video direction for bands like Linkin Park, Iggy Pop and John Frusciante, as well as for the photo shoots he has worked on for magazines such as *i-D*, *Dazed & Confused* and

Another Magazine. The initial idea for Fucking Awesome was to create clothing that both Mike and Jason wanted to wear and give to their friends, and was created from a mixture of boredom and excessive creativity and illegal substances to become one of the most sought-after streetwear clothing brands in the world. Jason still lives in New York, but Mike moved back to Los Angeles, which has helped to create

hype on both sides of the American market, something most brands never achieve. Fucking Awesome have now introduced full Spring/Summer and Fall/Winter collections. Mike answers some questions here.

How did you get involved in streetwear, and when?
It was by accident and I still feel uncomfortable stating that I am involved in street culture. I don't

▼▼ ▼▼ Spring/Summer, 2007

think we ever wanted to be involved in any culture besides the one that was our lives. Dill and I lived in a loft on Canal Street and we tried to outdo each other through our consumption of different substances that led to what is now each season of our bad ideas. When we started it was really just us printing fifteen shirts in our apartment for our friends. It was 2000–01 and 'streetwear' was not a phrase we would ever use. Dill being Dill gave us the opportunity to get lots of free shit and then we started filling in the holes by making the stuff we wanted to wear that no one else was making.

Where do streetwear's strengths and weaknesses lie?

I think that they're one and the same thing. Over the past few years, streetwear has exploded into a commodity similar to our neighbours in the X-treme world. With that, people are able to make more money to make more products like this book. They're also people with business degrees that will not sit back and ignore the fact that kids wait in lines to buy patent leather clown shoes. I am not an authority or a GLOBAL INFLUENCE but I read what's going on and it baffles me.

◀▼ Spring/Summer, 2006   ▼ Autumn/Winter, 2005   ▼▼ Spring/Summer, 2006

Where is streetwear going?
In circles. As things grow beyond the street onto the internet and into the suburbs, you have a new audience. Then more brands pop up due to the current demand for the super limited whatever. We now have an over-saturated market. So with that, a new group of dissatisfied twenty-somethings who have big ideas and access to a computer will probably come up with their own thing that will catch on to start the circle all over again.

The key to success in business is longevity. How do you see this in relation to streetwear and how do you apply it to your design work and business development?
Continue to make stuff that we want to wear and see if anyone else will buy it. Dill and I both have careers outside of t-shirts and jeans that affords us the option of failure. The fact that we can make whatever we want and not have to follow any trend forecast for fear of keeping the doors open may be enough.

▼▼ ▼▶ Spring/Summer, 2006

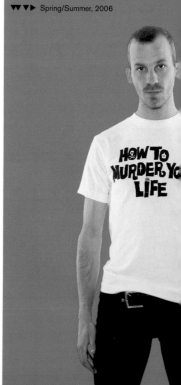

Founded by: **Erik Brunetti**
When: **1990**
Where: **Los Angeles, USA**
Website: **www.fuct.com**

For the past fifteen years, Erik Brunetti has been busy building, and re-building, the FUCT empire. It all began when his uncle pulled him out of high school, assuring young Erik that his path in life was as an artist. He took various design jobs and was fired from them in Modena (for asking his employer's daughter out on a date), in Pomona (after attempting to set fire to the indoor parking lot of his office), at The Morning Call in Alpha (for his religious beliefs) and in Verona, where the bridal magazine he was making layouts for filed for bankruptcy. So he decided to give up design for a while. In 1984, he moved to New York and worked as a bicycle messenger by day, and wandered the streets and train stations as a graffiti writer by night. He eventually made his mark in the burgeoning, yet still underground,

graffiti scene. His first real success as a freelance designer came when he moved to California and began making skateboard artwork. In 1990, he teamed up with Sev to make the first ever graffiti-art skateboard graphic. Later that year, Brunetti created FUCT, which soon earned him a reputation as one of the toughest streetwear designers in America.

Since then, he has created t-shirt graphics inspired by *Planet Of The Apes*, Vietnam, the Second World War, Rock 'n' Roll icons and the mob. He has reappropriated corporate logos, political ideologies from the 1960s to the present day, as well as popular contemporary artworks, only to twist them into the uniquely subversive designs that FUCT is renowned for.

Author Steven Vogel and Elle Rosenthal spoke to Brunetti:

This interview was hammered out and stitched together over three months on the road, mostly in Joshua Tree and Los Angeles, Tijuana and Arizona. As I write this, we are in Allentown, Pennsylvania, where heavy fog warnings are out, and we are up against a deadline that has a cursing Brunetti locked in a farmhouse on the most isolated road of this town.

We're well into our thirtieth hour now and Brunetti is working and talking to himself, and I think I just heard him say, 'The rest will have to be done by God', which may mean he is finished.

This long project began on a beach in Mexico where we went with Brunetti to begin taping. The first time I started recording, we were standing in the ocean with water to our waists, fully clothed. The *National Journal* had just published a detailed account on Karl Rove's (President Bush's chief political adviser) caution to other White House aides that Bush's 2004 re-election prospects would be damaged if it was disclosed he had been personally warned that a key rationale for going to war had been challenged within the administration. Brunetti was sucking up margaritas as he commented: 'Even if Bush does get impeached, it doesn't prove the system works. You still have to wonder how such a sophisticated criminal got his foot into the White House in the first place.'

SV: You just paid as much for your morning paper as you might have for a good pile of dope. Are you a news junkie, now?

EB: Yeah, I must have the news. One of these mornings, I'm gonna buy a paper with a big black headline that says, 'George Bush Committed Suicide Last Night'. Can you imagine that rush?

SV: Do you get off on politics the same way you used to on drugs?

EB: It depends on the politics, or the drugs. There are different kinds of highs. I had this discussion in San Felipe one night with a girl who wanted me to get stoned with her for about ten days on the finest prescription pills to be had in all of Mexico. But I told her I couldn't: I had to be back in LA.

SV: That doesn't exactly fit your image as the drug-crazed outlaw artist. Are you saying you'd rather have been in your loft downtown, working on graphics and listening to Crosby, Stills & Nash than stoned on the beach with a girl?

EB: Well – it depends on the timing. On Wednesday, I might want to stay in LA; on Thursday, I might want to go to Mexico.

SV: What do you like best?

EB: Probably food and sex. When you get into fine gastronomy like Boeuf Bourguignon and soufflés, it's a clear kind of high, an interior high. But really, when you're dealing with sex, there's only one pure pleasure for me, and that's French Shibari. I discovered this pleasant way of spending time on a trip to Paris. The beauty of it is that all you need is your wife and ten feet of rope.

SV: You drink a little, too, don't you?

EB: Obviously, but you notice I very rarely sit down and say, 'Now I'm going to get wasted.' I never eat a tremendous amount of any one thing either. I rarely get drunk and I smoke cigarettes the same way.

SV: Do you think the feds are watching, with all the things you've printed on t-shirts since FUCT made it's first public appearance?

EB: Of course. They're probably hiding in the bushes like wolverines. I have no choice but to work out of secret locations. I used to have my laundry delivered to my sister's house and have my friend Linda pick it up. Then I'd send an intern in to Linda's and have him drop it off at my neighbour's apartment. But things kept on disappearing all the time, so I stopped doing that.

SV: You say your style and ideas have been borrowed by a few other streetwear brands. How do you feel about this?

EB: Well, none of them have offered to pay my rent yet. That kind of unacknowledged dishonesty deserves to be exposed to the generations of streetwear fans who buy into these meaningless products devoid of any sense of values – except commercial value of course! – and that convey a monotone message of cultural ignorance, all in the name of fashion. It's eye candy. But don't get me wrong: there is nothing evil about eye candy when it does not presume to be anything else but something that is most remarkable by it's visual appearance. What makes me cringe is decoration that is passed off as art. To be more specific: FUCT's designs and ideas, which are reappropriated and repackaged into some insignificant object, and sold to kids as something magnificently original and revolutionary.

SV: Yes, but who?

EB: Well, certain people used to hang around our store on Beverly Boulevard. They were very sneaky. No one knew they had the intention of starting their own clothing line or would blatantly rip off FUCT's ideas. Suddenly a certain store awning included a logo that I designed for FUCT (a piece inspired by the 1970s version of *King Kong*). Years later, I decided to take one of this guy's designs and purposely reappropriated it to give him a taste of his own medicine. Sure enough, he sent a fax saying something about dumping me in the east river (laughing). I don't understand that kind of heathen behaviour. I mean why didn't he call me on the phone after his first big break and thank me for giving him a career? That would have been the proper thing to do, don't you think?

SV: Talk me through what has happened.

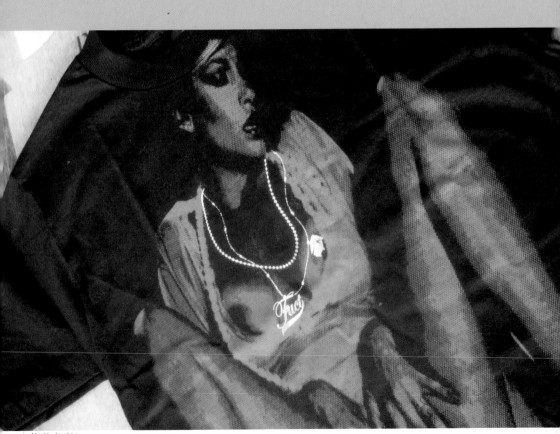

▲ Untitled t-shirt
◄ Selection of graphics

▶ Untitled t-shirt

EB: People would send FUCT packages of, say, sticker art. They wanted our store to carry their stuff. But we were only carrying FUCT and XLARGE at the time. One person in particular is a very nice guy – we have had pleasant conversations in the past. I even own three or four of his prints. They make fantastic decorative posters, I just don't think he realizes certain things. He and I are two different people, apparently drinking out of the same bowl of water. At first, I'd say to myself that imitation was probably the finest form of flattery. But I have to say, seeing your ideas reappear under another person's credit is not exactly thrilling. I spend a lot of time reading about things, researching them and fine-tuning my art. When, say, someone prints a profile of Mao Zedong – the same profile of Mao Zedong that FUCT cleverly borrowed to symbolize the Asian devil – and does so several seasons later, portraying the genocide genius as some kind of revolutionary, what do you think all the smart kids were thinking? Let alone the Chinese kids? Hell, he might as well have printed a zillion Hitler silk-screens and wheat-pasted them all over.

SV: So what is the meaning of 'street' then? Surely, I would think this brand has earned that credibility. It's on the streets everywhere.

EB: Yes, true. But did he wheat-paste all those himself? No, he didn't. That's the difference between a graffiti bomber and a 'sticker bomber'. I loathe it when publications call that art graffiti, or bombing. It's not. Tagging on public property can become a felony and in some cities it actually is. Posting stickers and flyers on public property is barely a misdemeanour. But what I truly find absurd is 'illegal' street art in a gallery. When any form of street art is transposed into a gallery context, it loses practically all of it's meaning. Part of what makes this art form different from other forms is the landscape it is presented in, pieces and tags showing up everywhere and anywhere, it is a pure message of expression, but once it is displayed as decoration in a gallery, it loses its impact and content. It's just aerosol on a canvas. Where is the statement?

SV: Interesting point.

EB: That's why I say that the meaning of 'street' is long lost. It's not about re-enforcing the need for over-consumption by making kids and grown men buy shitloads of useless collectible toys that stay sealed in their boxes. It's about self-expression and the desire to belong to a movement or a cause: something bigger than life. Not bigger than your wallet. No $90

t-shirt that pretends to advocate rebellion can truly stand the test of time. A printed t-shirt costs about $4 to make. Printed, folded and wrapped. So, you do the math. If encouraging lavish life-styles of the rich and famous is what you wish to do, then continue handing over your cash to the Bentley-driving, disc-jockey-improvising 'streetwear' conglomerates of this world. But trying to explain this to anyone who hasn't figured it out on his own.

SV: Well, you certainly say some outrageous things.

EB: If you listen carefully to what I say, you'll notice that these are mere facts. The only outrageous thing is the amount of ideas that have been stolen over the years.

SV: Is it true you were threatened via fax?

EB: Correct. Streetwear used to actually be 'dangerous'. It's all quite comical. I think a shirt that reads: 'Monkey see, Monkey do' would be appropriate for these guys that got on the ape bandwagon late.

SV: Who are you referring to?

EB: I am referring to every clothing company in the world that did Vietnam or Kiss imagery after FUCT. We created and pioneered those crazes. My partner at the time and I were both on heavy drugs, we truly were fucked. We didn't realize that what we were creating at the time would have such a strong impact because no one was doing it at that time. We were addressing a social commentary of sorts by appropriating the *Planet Of The Apes* and Vietnam images. Such images provoked certain feelings and emotions when you saw a film still from them transposed in a new context. We didn't think about lawsuits. We would just consume pop culture of yesteryears, and redesign it as ours, as FUCT. When a company comes along after the fact, and does the same thing we are doing, in essence they are just lapping up our vomit and regurgitating an already digested idea. It is no longer art by commentary at this point, it is null and void of any credibility. It's just a stolen idea. However, FUCT was not the first company to use a simian as their logo or as graphics on t-shirts and posters. XLARGE did it first, with their company logo: it had a gorilla on it. Later we teamed up with them and did X-FUCT, and juxtaposed a psychotic-looking baby ape with human eyes. Thus, the X-FUCT graphic was born.

SV: You mentioned being on heavy drugs. Can you explain?

EB: I will only speak for myself. The X-FUCT warehouse was a fucking party zone. H. R. from Bad Brains was living in our loft, hiding out from his band mates. MCA (the Beastie Boys) was trying to convince him to pull it together and regroup. Rick Ocasek (the Cars) was there. Even Madonna, who wanted to sign Bad Brains on Maverick at the time, would stop by.

SV: So, no more drugs now?

EB: Yeah. That party has been over for a while. It was a different time then, we where figuring it out as we went along, none of us had degrees in business. I remember Slick and I both trying to figure out how to use the cash register one day. FUCT got known by accident, that's what makes it great. We had no plans for the future, we had no biz strategy, we just charged full speed ahead.

SV: You also mentioned a partner?

EB: Yes, Slick. I met him through the graffiti scene. We were doing pieces together. I was already doing FUCT and decided to team up with him. He's an amazing illustrator. So I figured both of our skills combined would be unstoppable. Until we encountered creative differences and drugs became part of the game. It wasn't long before the split.

SV: What's this I heard about guns and biker gangs involved in the split?

EB: No comment.

SV: Your artistic style has been attacked by critics – most notably, on internet blogs – partly commentary, partly fantasy but mostly the ravings of someone too long into drugs. What are your thoughts?

EB: Do you believe everything you read on the internet? They obviously spend their days following me around and watching my every move. All this internet-as-entertainment has given these sneaker and toy collectors a soapbox to stand on and spew about how I am a 'H8ter'. I don't hate anyone. I am a very thoughtful, warm-hearted person. Everyday, I spread the gospel of love and truth. So to answer your question: it's kind of endearing when people devote so much of their time and energy to you. I imagine them sitting in their carefully organized bedrooms, with all their carefully organized sneakers and action figures, sitting in front of their computers, obsessing over useless shit. Internet blogs are very similar to soap operas. Somewhat entertaining, but always dramatically deficient and cheap. I love it.

SV: Are there any companies you do like? Recent companies?

EB: Topshelf Motherfucker. I like those guys.

SV: What inspires you these days? I read in *i-D* a few years back that the 'news' on TV inspires you. I believe you said CNN to be exact?

EB: That's correct. I love the news. As I said earlier, I'm a news junkie. *The Los Angeles Times*, Newsweek, CNN. It's interesting to study the inherent biases of journalism – especially on television. Because there is no such thing as an objective point of view.

SV: What's coming up for your next collection?

EB: I had this vision of Freddie Mercury and Richey James Edwards.

SV: When you sit down to start designing, what is your process?

EB: I read a lot. Every day I take in my surroundings and think about them, and I try to find images that convey those surroundings and thoughts.

SV: Do you ever wonder how you have survived this long? You are thirty-eight now, correct?

EB: Yes, that's correct. I don't think anybody expected me to get much past thirty-two years old. Least of all me. I guess I always just assumed that this concrete idea was only somewhat grounded in truth but now it all seems to make sense. This is a marvellous yet very imitative world; you can't afford to let the copycats off the hook that easily. You have to keep on going and give it all you've got. You want to keep your benefactors close and your dead ringers even closer. But first and foremost, you really want to apply the principles of Love Awareness at all times.

◀▶ Untitled t-shirts

Founded by: **Hiroshi Fujiwara**
When: **2005 (Honeyee.com)**
Where: **Tokyo, Japan**
Websites: **www.fragment.jp www.honeyee.com**

There are many names, or idioms, that Hiroshi goes by in the streetwear world. Many call him 'the most influential designer', while others refer to him as 'the godfather of streetwear' or 'the father of Japanese streetwear'. As Jeff Staple puts it: 'Hiroshi Fujiwara is your favourite tastemaker's favourite tastemaker.' It is hard to describe any more succinctly the extent of Hiroshi's influence on the streetwear industry, especially because only a few of the people involved in the subculture are fully aware of it. Apart from design, Hiroshi has worked as a DJ, a producer and a musician, not only in Japan, but worldwide. In 2006, he worked on a joint release with Eric Clapton and designed for the seminal guitar company, Martin.

Hiroshi has designed some of the most coveted brands in the streetwear world, including Nike and Idiom, which is well-known for creating technically advanced yet stylish snowboard wear. He also runs his own Levi's line in Japan (called Fenom), and regularly collaborates with other designers to create offshoot items like the AFFA (Anarchy Forever, Forever Anarchy) products with Jun Takahashi. He is responsible for the much sought-after brand, GoodEnough, and also started the online magazine honeyee.com. This has become one of the most widely read streetwear websites, especially the blog, through which he invited friends and co-workers to share their thoughts and ideas with the world.

What does the term streetwear mean to you?

I can't identify with what streetwear is being defined as today, for example the t-shirt fascination and skateboard-orientated crowds of kids. To me, streetwear came from the punk days, which was a real alternative underground culture, out of which a certain dress style manifested itself.

How did you get involved in the streetwear scene and when?

It was around 1977 when I started taking a real interest in punk. Afterwards, as I became more deeply involved in the underground culture, it was things like skateboarding and especially Stüssy, that embodied a lot of what I was thinking and feeling at the time.

Where do streetwear's strengths and weaknesses lie?

One of its undeniable strengths is that it has underground power. By that I mean it is unpredictable and cannot be packaged and marketed for the masses. I think the biggest weakness it has is keeping the balance between being underground and genuine, and then trying to make a living out of it. That is what most people struggle with in this subculture – trying to remain small and underground, and yet at the same time making enough money to live.

Where do you think streetwear is going?

Unfortunately, I think right now this subculture is becoming much more mainstream than it has ever been and as a result, a lot of the people like myself are no longer interested in it.

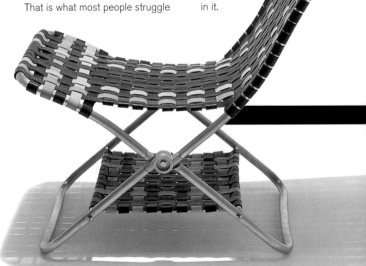

So what is more interesting to you at the moment?

In terms of the underground movement there isn't anything interesting to me, as there doesn't seem to be an underground movement right now. It is difficult at the moment to build any sort of underground movement because of the internet. The information moves too quickly and anything new doesn't get the proper time any more to let it grow organically. Right now for me anyway, I am picking up things in different places and genres that interest me. They don't necessarily have to be from a company that is any way related to this scene, or have a philosophy of streetwear, or are products that are in any way related to it at all. It's more like a mix and match process at the moment, which realistically it has always been anyway. Mix and match, or appropriation of several ideas and then making something new, is the root of this subculture. For example if you look at the punk phenomena, or any kind of movement, like Mods or whatever. That was one thing I always really liked about Stüssy, was that they always appropriated designs from people like Comme de Garçon or Agnès B and made them their own in a very good way.

What is the essence of streetwear?

I don't think you can think of the essence in terms of a label or brand. I think it's definitely all

▲ AFFA TYPE MA-1 CUSTOM jacket, early 1990s
◀ Woven concept folding chair, 2002

cotton base
GOODENOUGH-T-SHIRT-SIZE-S

cotton base
GOODENOUGH-T-SHIRT-SIZE-M

cotton base
GOODENOUGH-T-SHIRT-SIZE-L

cotton base
GOODENOUGH-T-SHIRT-SIZE-XL

gdeh

ʼIVINGᵈ GOODLIVINGᵈ
ᵈUᵈH ᵈᵈᵈᵈᵈENOUᵈH

ʼs good Enough

goodenoug

GOODENOUGH

GEᐧ IMPROVISATION

GDEH
G-WEATHERPROOF FOR MO

GEᐧ IMPROVISATION

G-WEATHERPROOF F

GOODEN

GᴇGᴇ
GOODENOUGH 2001

▲ A selection of graphics
◄ Head Porter Guarantee Card, 1998

▲▲▲ HF Kubrick promotion toy (*Slash Magazine*), 2000

GᴇGᴇ

about the attitude of the group as well as the taste and attitude of the designer that defines the essence. This subculture is all about individuals contributing to one big pot.

Which memorable events had an impact on your life?

One of the most memorable and important things, not only for myself, but the whole of Tokyo, was when Stüssy first came here in the 1980s. Shawn Stüssy, Michael Kopelman and Alex and everyone else from New York, LA and London all came here together. It was the first time that everyone came together here. The best thing that came out of that was the international Stüssy tribe, which is how I made friends with Paul Mittleman, Michael Kopelman and all that.

What do you like the most about streetwear?

One aspect I have come to appreciate recently, even though I did say that it is one of this culture's weaknesses, is the internet. I am really fascinated about how you can share information nowadays. The ability to communicate with

people all over the world so easily and regularly. In the 1980s and 1990s you had to travel and meet people, which is a good thing of course, but today you can connect to people daily with the push of a button. Sure, it is a little impersonal because you are 'talking' to a screen, but I still find it amazing. Sometimes I think that anonymity of the internet is quite good.

With special thanks to Fraser Cooke

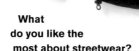

▲ Head Porter + Mountain Parka, 2001
◀▶ Martin acoustic guitar #839775, 2002

GIMME5

Founded by: **Michael Kopelman**
When: **1990s**
Where: **London, UK**
Websites: **www.stussy.com**
www.hideoutstore.com
www.foot-patrol.com
www.benwilsondesign.co.uk

▶ Honda x Stüssy Zoomer. Photos by James Pearson Howes
  Graphics by Studio Oscar www.studiooscar.com

Wtaps, Neighborhood, Gimme5, Unrivalled, Acronym, anything, Headporter, Resonate, Original Fake, Tonite, Surrender and BBC. In addition, Gimme5 runs and operates four stores (Stüssy, The Hideout, Foot Patrol and Busy Work Shop (BAPE) – (BAPE)'s only European flagship store). Gimme5 was founded and run by Michael Kopelman, and over the past two decades, his vision and determination have laid the ground for many of the things that are now taken for granted in today's subculture. It was Kopelman's idealism that brought the majority of the Japanese streetwear labels, as well as Stüssy – commonly believed to have kickstarted streetwear culture – to Europe. And as if distributing and retailing wasn't enough for Kopelman, he also runs his own labels, Goodenough UK and Gimme5, through which he has worked with many artists.

Gimme5 is an enigma, despite its incredible contribution to the UK and European streetwear scene. As an umbrella company, it distributes and sells brands such as Stüssy, Visvim, Goodenough UK, Supreme,

How and when did you get involved in streetwear?

I went to California to see Shawn (Stüssy). I knew Paul Mittleman, since he had been over a few times and he was working with Shawn. I met him on a DJ tour in Japan. I then re-met Hiroshi Fujiwara: we previously met in Camden buying the same records. I had some severance money and I started my own t-shirt/distribution company called Gimme5.

What best represents your work?

Probably one of my most recent collaborations with Stüssy UK and designer Ben Wilson, where we worked on a Honda chopper, creating the Honda x Stüssy Zoomer.

What is streetwear?

What people wear every day.

What is your work philosophy?

My work is a fashion business, not science or medicine or a philosophy.

▲▶ Honda x Stüssy Zoomer. Photos by James Pearson Howes, Graphics by Studio Oscar www.studiooscar.com

THE HUNDREDS

Founded by: **Bobby & Ben Hundreds**
When: **2003**
Where: **Los Angeles, USA**
Website: **www.thehundreds.com**

LOS ANGELES
the
Hundreds

The Hundreds is a two-part project, which includes a clothing line and a website. The website is an online magazine devoted to the streetwear subculture and includes Bobby and Ben's blog, which is enhanced by contributions from other members of The Hundreds team and driven by original content and an honest approach to the subject matter. Thanks to a history of involvement in the Californian skate and music scene, the website is not only relevant but entertaining too, and enhances the impact of The Hundreds's main project, a clothing line influenced by the 1980s and 1990s subculture of southern California. Bobby and Ben's integrity, inventiveness and open-minded approach to streetwear has helped The Hundreds to become one of the most influential streetwear brands in the world. Bobby comments below:

Followers of the 'Old School' by Bobby Hundreds

A few months ago in an interview, I was asked how it felt to be one of the 'Leaders of the New School.' *Leaders*? Uhh … Of the *New School*? Wha..? Because, correct me if I'm wrong, but I wasn't aware that the 'Old School' had run its course. Correct me if I'm wrong, but isn't the 'Old School' still leading the way for us all?

▲▲▲▲▲ Fall/Winter, 2006

Ben and I started The Hundreds here in Los Angeles three years ago. But The Hundreds started decades ago, somewhere amidst rudimentary crayon drawings and graphite doodles on desktops. Drawing came naturally (both my parents being artists), but I had no interest in realism or exactness. Growing up in the 1980s, my life was consumed with the surreal and absurd: the exaggerated curves and bulging characteristics of Saturday morning cartoons, Garfield comic strips and Calvin and Hobbes.

So when I was eight years old, and T&C Surf, Maui & Sons and B.A. proliferated beach culture stateside with their fluorescent cartoon graphics on white t-shirts, I fell in love with wearable art.

When I was ten years old, Stüssy, Mossimo and Freshjive picked up where the surf labels had left off by infusing everything 'street' – skateboarding, hip hop or the rave scene – with Southern Cali flavour. The result? Loud cartoonized parodies, bold corporate graphic flips and oversized logos. And plenty of eager niche consumers like me, trading in my baseball cards and comic books for limited t-shirts.

By the time I turned twelve, the near-flatlined skate industry had taken a cue from the early streetwear pioneers (or was it the other way round?) and mom-n-pop skateshops lined their racks with colourful graphic t-shirts by indie skateboard companies. In contrast to mass-produced skate t-shirts you

find in mall souvenir shops today, the early 1990s skateboarding culture was a breeding ground for some of the most creative and influential t-shirt graphics ever produced. And if you were lucky enough to find that exclusive Blind 'Bye Bye Kitty,' SCS 'Brat' or Color 'Bear' jump-off, there wasn't a chance in hell you'd see another kid within a three school-district radius who'd match.

It's 1998 and my first week interning at *Warp Magazine*. My editor has me call up every skate company imaginable to request product samples for our quarterly column. After breezing through pages of 949s, 619s and 760s, I hit a 212 phone number. 'Supreme? In New York? Just call 'em,' Kevin

▲ Fall/Winter, 2006

shouts from behind the wall. Some kid with a Brooklyn accent picks up. 'Hey, this is Bobby with *Warp Magazine.*' He laughs in my face under three seconds flat, and I'm left with a dialtone.

Over the next few years, I'd save up my money to visit New York as much as possible. Not because I craved curbside roasted nuts, but because I had to be the only one in my circle of friends who had a legitimate box-logo t-shirt purchased on Lafayette. The only one with original first-series Alife slip-ons, and that SSUR hoody I had seen in Japanese magazines.

And as long as I was reading Japanese magazines, why not go to Japan? There I consumed/researched/observed Bape, NBHD,

Wtaps and every other covert label that had missed my radar back home in Shopping Mall Land. I became a fan. I liked this stuff because I liked the design, but just as importantly, the people behind the brands, their vision and their hustle. I admired the anti-corporate/anti-sellout approach to business. I appreciated the unique product, the limited distribution and the special sense of owning something exclusive, personally constructed by peers who shared my respect and admiration for this culture.

I came home and Ben and I started The Hundreds. Since day one, we have been following the unwritten business model that the first generation laid before us. We stick to the blueprint, although

we interpret it our own way, and gear it towards our generation. We do our best to educate the community on the game and the players involved, although in reality, we are more students than teachers.

It's 2006 and I'm twenty-six years old. Somehow, I am fortunate enough to pay my bills off doing something I love. Even if I didn't end up in this line of work, I'd still have the same daily routine, wear the same clothes, shop at the same stores, read the same magazines and respect the same people who have paid their dues and have built the bridges. As long as we do this, we will always recognize and respect the forefathers. We will always be Followers. Followers of the Old School.

IN4MATION

Founded by: **Ryan Arakaki, Jun Jo, Rhandy Tambio & Todd Shimabuku** (essay by Todd Shimabuku)
When: **2002**
Where: **Mililani, Hawaii**
Website: **www.in4mants.com**

In4mation is a clothing brand and store from a region in the world that isn't well known for its street culture. On the contrary, Hawaii is synonymous with golf courses and surfing rather than sneakers and street culture, and one would presume that its geographical isolation would make it difficult for an urban subculture to evolve. Yet despite the odds, Hawaii has a strong and healthy streetwear scene that can perhaps in part be attributed to its physical location – right in the middle of the two streetwear meccas, Los Angeles and Tokyo.

Todd Shimabuku and his three partners opened their first store in 2002 and subsequently expanded the business to include a second store in 2005, as well as creating their own brand, in4mation. In4mation quickly developed worldwide renown for its original, challenging, high quality and entertaining design approach. It is also internationally relevant thanks to convincing collaborations with designers such as Marok, the publisher of *Lodown* magazine, as well as *Methamphibian*. In addition to creating several great t-shirts, in4mation have also produced

complete clothing lines and sneakers, working with brands such as èS Footwear.

What sets in4mation apart from the t-shirt labels popping up around the world is that their products reflect a genuine approach to, and appreciation of, streetwear. In the following essay entitled 'difference?', Todd writes here about streetwear and outlines his experiences:

Looking at how our lives were, and how we were raised, has made me realize that this lucrative market has not only become one of the most sought-after monster markets but

▲ Army t-shirt   ▲ Guilty by Association t-shirt   ▲ Evil Monito collaboration t-shirt

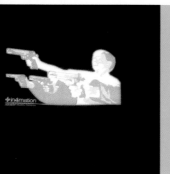

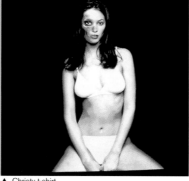

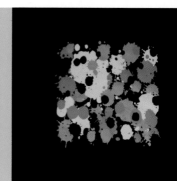

▲ Guns t-shirt   ▲ Christy t-shirt   ▲ Camo t-shirt

has actually brought a sense of a common bond in the majority of the people we have met over the years. I really feel that all eyes are on us and it is up to us to keep the monster guessing. The monster does not know about how hard it was to really find one's self individuality. By having a piece of clothing that made a statement more than just being a trend was the most fun part of being an ANTI person on my part. My partners and I were all into this sense and we all shared a common bond with music, hobbies and attitude. I remember when there were good concerts in Hawaii, there were actually good shows on every month. I would see that the people I have met while being there at, let's say a Bad Religion, Pantera,

White Zombie, Pennywise or even a Beastie Boys gig, would be the kind of people I would relate to in the long run. I look at how they would not care about society's rules and said fuck it. THIS IS WHO I AM. You would see it all, the jarheads, the MOKES (Polynesian dudes who were at every punk show because they thought the PIT was meant for fighting), punks, druggies and the older guys in the Beer Garden who I thought were the coolest guys in the world. The word 'common' comes into play again as you go back to school and talk about your experiences towards the people you have seen at the concerts and functions, and it's like instant acceptance towards each party. IF YOU LIKE THE MUSIC I LIKE

… YOU'RE COOL! Concerts were somewhere you could be free and dress however you wanted to: shipwreck pants with some old Sals or Chukkas and a white t-shirt. PERFECT!!!

Getting older, as the surf crowd in Hawaii got into punk, the surfers were just jumping on the skate bandwagon and it made me turn away from the whole punk scene. I looked at hip hop and would hear a lot of it from a friend who I can pretty much call my brother in skateboarding. I was taught about A Tribe Called Quest and the Native Tongues. This was not normal-sounding rap music. Learning more about this made me quit skateboarding and start researching the emergence of hip hop.

▲ Misfits t-shirt

▲ In4mation logo t-shirt

▲ Respect locals t-shirt

▲ Blood logo t-shirt

▲ Girl logo t-shirt

▲ Hard to Earn t-shirt

Learning about production, reading the linear notes on the tape/CD sleeves, looking who has affiliation so I could look into what's next. The Gangstarr Foundation and D&D Studios have brought us the most classic music because they were living the lifestyle. Looking at guys like Natas Kaupas with his Public Enemy t-shirts and Skids pants kind of made hip hop look more underground. Seeing a live DJ at a local skate contest with him playing the hits has only made me look at music as something with power in involvement. Hearing a guy play a record and mixing with some cuts got me into what hip hop was about: the preservation of a culture. Buying a couple of Technics 12s, I eventually got into being a buyer of hip hop vinyl records. There was no way of getting 'that dude', meaning RECORD EXECUTIVES, to accept your music unless you were accepted! The struggle continues and a movement is still there but you can't voice your opinion if you're trying to keep your voice low and only keeping your audience targeted towards the underground.

Hip hop was never accepted like skateboarding and was always looked down upon, but look at it now in 2006! You have hip hop/punk/rock&roll/skate/surf personas exploited into a lifestyle that was created by our people who fought for something they believed in. STREETWEAR!!!!

I am fortunate to have been through a broken home with the freedom that was given to me. I was lucky to be able to do the things that I have done that made me think differently. Being the only one in my graduating class that loved school but looked like I didn't; it's still the same story when I see a classmate and they ask 'So what do you do now?' My response 'I just work and I love it!' If there were no difference in the way we were there would be no STREETWEAR. I am turning thirty-one soon and I still feel like I was when I was in high school. To this day I try to be different because everything is getting popular.

▲ Shop logo t-shirt
◄ Mobster t-shirt

139

INVISIBLE
MAN

▲▲▲ Untitled Spring/Summer 2006 t-shirts

Streetwear is a manifestation of a person's lifestyle at a particular time, which has produced a multi-faceted subculture, now almost impossible to explain in its entirety. Well, almost. It could be argued that no one embodies the true meaning of streetwear more than Andrew Lee. With his brand, invisible: man, Andrew leads and shapes the streetwear subculture like no other. His clothing collections have achieved cult status across the world, and he has worked as a freelance designer for brands such as Stüssy, Neighborhood, the Japanese skateboard company T-19, realmadHectic and Kinetics, as well as footwear companies like èS and Madfoot. His work is even recognized by the couture world, thanks to his attention to detail, high production standards and his ability to predict and set trends.

Streetwear is a relatively new term for something that most people either don't, or can't, define. Yet there seems to be a collective understanding about what it is, and especially what it is not. How do you define it?
Well, I think it's just another buzz word in the same vein as ALTERNATIVE (rock), or ESPN bastardizing EXTREME. It's rather clever you're using it as the title

Founded by: **Andrew Lee** When: **1999** Where: **New York & LA, USA & Tokyo, Japan** Website: **www.newevil.com**

of this book, because by the end of the book, after one has seen all the amazing art, design and actual original thought and themes included, 'streetwear' as a scene or title, faction or institution will have been completely demolished. I have no definition of that word when it comes down to it. I know what it is, but I don't want to limit myself or what I do to just that. Yet some base their entire existence around it.

When did you realize you were involved in something special?
I watched hip hop, skateboarding, bmx, punk and other fads and trends, but I've never considered it 'special'. I think what did change my point of view, was the amount of money all these people I thought were soulful, simple-living artistic geniuses were making, like god damn, I love this, and LIVE this stuff, and I can make a living too?

I just figured I'd have this little creative thing as a side dish. But instead, I chose to do it for a career.

Where do streetwear's strengths and weaknesses lie?
There's a lot of backstabbing and shit talking, which there is in everything. I embrace it, because I love a good scandal, but friends stabbing friends is a bit too much and I think everyone copying

▲ Untitled Spring/Summer 2006 t-shirts

everyone is pretty shitty. But there are so many good people in this game, so many amazingly gifted people, and people are noticing it – just look at Gucci and Burberry and Louis Vuitton and all those 'high-fashion brands' that are supposed to be cutting edge and world renowned: they rob and steal everything we do. No really, go look – we must be doing something right.

What memorable events had an impact on you, and then on streetwear as a subculture?

The friendships I have acquired over the years have had the biggest impact. Are you asking me what I have contributed? If anything, I'm the bastard you want to beat the shit out of, but you can't because I'm fucking RIGHT, and you know it.

The key to success is longevity. How do you apply this to your business?

Well I've learned a few really good lessons business-wise: mostly that people's promises are bullshit, and for the most part, everyone is out for themselves. So as we speak, I am destroying and rebuilding everything I've done so far, and it's exciting. No matter how I want to quit this bullshit and go work at Costco, I can't. I guess I'm not done yet. I have a lot more buttons to push.

Where is streetwear going?

I signed a confidentially agreement, I'm not at liberty to comment.

In recent years, focus has shifted onto the product itself, and away from other elements of this subculture (such as skateboarding, music, etc.). How do you explain that, and what do you think of this development?

Nobody gives a fuck about the product, people concentrate on the hype, on the coverage, on which moron with a record deal wears it, and it's sad, because a lot of the time, the corniest shit and the crappiest brands are celebrated, leaving the brands they stole their 'hot designs' from in the shadows. Which makes me laugh inside, because after all these years, after everyone's blood, sweat and tears, and dedication to their craft and commitments to bust ass to create the most amazing products and lifestyles known to man, the mainstream consumers and media players and the pushers of this dope just don't and won't ever understand our extreme, alternative generation X, streetwear world. Just play some Slayer records, read a book, go ride a skateboard or go swimming. Get the fuck away from your computers and blogs: there's a whole world outside. But yeah, you might get those sneakers dirty. Nevermind.

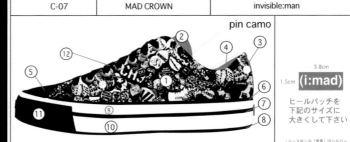

STYLE NO.	STYLE NANE.	COLOR
C-07	MAD CROWN	invisible:man

pin camo

3.8cm

1.5cm **(i:mad)**

ヒールパッチを
下記のサイズに
大きくして下さい

・レースホール（金具）はシルバー
・ソール底カラーBLACK
・インソールはBLACK
・RED COLOR/PANTONE 485 CVC

PARTS	MATERIALS	COLOR	OTHERS
UPPER			
1. BLKのサイド部分	オリジナルキャンバス	WHITE BASE	
		ステッチはBLACK	
2. タン	キャンバス	RED	
		ロックステッチBKACK	
3. ヒールテープ	キャンバス	RED	※版が微妙に変わってるので
		ステッチRED（同色）	新たにおこして下さい
4. ライニング	キャンバス	キャンバス色	
5. 爪先のキャップ	ラバー	BLACK	
		WHITE	
SOLE			
6. ライン（上）	ラバー	BLACK	
7. ライン（下）	ラバー	BLACK	
8. アウトソール	ラバー	BLACK	
9. ミッドソール（上）	ラバー	WHITE	
10. ミッドソール（下）	ラバー	WHITE	
11. 爪先部分	ラバー	BLACK	
ACCESSARY			
12. シューレース	ラバー	WHITE	
		スペアにBLK	

SAMPLE SIZE

10 INCH

MOULD

QUANTITY

ORDER DATE

DROW UP (作成日)

2005.12.21

◀▲ Madfoot x invisible:man sneaker

JB
CLASSICS

Founded by: **Jason Bass**   When: **2002**   Where: **San Francisco, USA**   Website: **www.suite2206.com**

Jason Bass is the one-man army behind one of the most original independent footwear companies today. It all started with a dream to unite his artworks with a fascination and obsession with sneakers, and so he set up a business in 2002 in San Francisco. It quickly caught the attention of like-minded individuals worldwide. Using a hands-on personal approach, Jason continues to design, glue, stitch and pack his shoes, constantly pushing the boundaries between art and sneakers. Jason is also part of the infamous KDU movement and recounts his story below with an individual twist:

Swoosh, swoosh, swoosh. Bounce, bounce, bounce. Sweak, sweak, sweak. The Little Sneaker rumbled over the ground. She was a happy Little Sneaker for she had such a soft feel to her insole. Her creativity was inspirational to all the boys and girls. There were bright colours, oval laces with lace locks and many materials, even some shiny ones. There were breath vents across the toe panel, tongues with nice logos and velcro straps. And the cleanest graphics you ever saw all over them. And there were tons of them, some had airbags, or bright colours, split-suede earth tones, genuine leather, even top premium nubuck and every kind of sneaker that the boys or girls could ever want.

But that was not all. Some of the uppers were covered with good things for the boys and girls to believe in: big AKs, naked women, red wrist watches, killer locusts, loan sharks, wild golden emus, and even special little tote bags for the boys and girls to put their boxes in.

The Little Sneaker was carrying all these great things for the boys and girls to the other side of the mountain. She puffed along so happily. Then all of a sudden she stopped with a jerk. She could not go another inch. She tried but her tread would not move.

What were all those good little boys and girls on the other side of the mountain going to do without the creative freedom and genuine material? What would they wear?

Here's comes a Shiny New Giant Venture Capitalist. Let's ask him to help us. 'Please carry me over the mountain, Shiny New Venture Capitalist. My sneaker is stuck and all the boys and girls on the other side will have no belief in creative freedom unless you help me,' cried the Little Sneaker.

But the Shiny New Giant Venture Capitalist snorted: 'Me help you? I only help low-risk brands. I have just carried a fine big brand over the mountain, with more distribution outlets than you could imagine.

◀▼ JB Wallabee

▲ JB Getlo Skeletors   ▲ JB Zen Garden
▲▼ JB Slips Piranhas   ▲ JB Globes

My firm has trade financing, production teams and PR connections. Me, help the likes of you? Indeed not!' And off he went to his winter house.

How sad the Little Sneaker felt. Then the Little Sneaker called out, 'The Shiny Giant Venture Capitalist isn't the only one in the world. Here comes a fine Big Strong Production House. Let's ask him to help us.'

The Little Sneaker waved her flag and the Big Strong Production House pulled up beside her. 'Please, oh, please, Big Strong Production House,' cried the Little Sneaker. 'Do pull us over the mountain. Our tread and laces are stuck and the good little boys and girls on the other side will have no idea of what creative freedom is unless you help us.'

But the Big Strong Production House bellowed, 'I only handle large quantities: my machines only handle ten thousand pairs at a time. I only make grown-up footwear. I am a

very important Production House. I won't help the likes of you!' And the Big Strong Production House turned away indignantly.

The Little Sneaker was very sad. 'Cheer Up!' cried out all the sneakers she was carrying, 'the Big Strong Production House is not the only one in the world. Here comes another one. He looks very old and tired, but our sneakers are small and light. Perhaps he can help us.'

So they waved their flag and the dingy, Rusty Old Banker stopped beside them. 'Please, Rusty Old Banker. Do pull our sneaker over the mountain. The boys and girls are waiting for all the creative freedom and inspiration. You have to help us!'

But the Rusty Old Banker sighed, 'I am so tired. I must rest my counting hands. I cannot even help the smallest of businesses over the mountain. I can't. I can't. I can't….' And off he rumbled, chugging, 'I can't. I can't. I can't.'

By this time, the Little Sneaker was very, very sad. But then she called out, 'Here comes another one. A Little Blue One, a very little one, but perhaps she will help us.'

The Little Blue One came chugging merrily along. When she saw the flag waving, she stopped quickly. 'What is the matter, my friends?' she asked kindly.

'Oh, Little Blue One,' cried the Little Sneaker, 'will you pull us over the mountain? Our tread and laces are stuck and all the boys and girls are waiting for us on the other side of the mountain. And they will be very upset, unless you can help us. Please help us, Little Blue One.'

'I'm not a very big,' said the Little Blue One. 'They only use me for bridging people together and I have never been over the mountain.'

'But we must get over the mountain before the children are upset,' replied the Little Sneaker. The Little Blue One looked up and saw the tears in the Little Sneaker's eyes. And she thought of all the good little boys and girls on the other side of the mountain that would not get to meet the Little Sneaker unless she helped. Then she said, 'I THINK I CAN. I THINK I CAN. I THINK I CAN!!!' And she attached herself to the Little Sneaker. She tugged and pulled and pulled and tugged and slowly, slowly, slowly started off.

Everyone began to cheer and smile as she puffed, puffed, puffed, chugged, chugged. 'I THINK I CAN, I THINK I CAN, I THINK I CAN!!!!!'

'Hurrah, Hurrah,' cried everyone. 'The good little boys and girls in the city will be happy because you helped us, kind Little Blue One.' And the Little Blue One smiled and seemed to say as she steadily puffed down the mountain, 'I THOUGHT I COULD, I THOUGHT I COULD, I THOUGHT I COULD.'

▲ JB Shirkens HI boots
▲ JB Getlos Loan Shark

Founded by: **Dave Gensler**
When: **2005**
Where: **New York, USA**
Websites: **www.thekdu.com www.theroyalmagazine.com**

The KDU (formally known as the Keystone Design Union) is an equal partnership programme, similar to an umbrella company, that develops, supports and manages streetwear designers and brands, as well as publishing *The Royal Magazine*. KDU represents brands such as JB Classics, Serum vs. Venom (SVSV). Dave manages all this, and runs *The Royal Magazine* too.

What's your background professionally and personally?
I am a designer and a brand strategist. I was born in Baltimore, Maryland and lived most of my life in Pennsylvania and California. I now live in New York, Williamsburg, Brooklyn to be precise. I spent ten years in the advertising and design service industry, developing solutions for some of the world's

largest brands. I founded my own firm in Philadelphia in 2000 called Human Brand. I then made the jump to the other side of the fence by becoming the Chief Brand Officer for all ROC brands, including Rocawear, Roc-A-Fella Records, Armadale Vodka, ROC Films and State Property. I then co-founded the KDU with Jason.

What do you do now?

I am the president of the KDU, as well as Editor-in-Chief of *The Royal Magazine* and Creative Director for SVSV.

What exactly does the KDU do?

The KDU functions on several unique platforms: we are a creative collective made up of some of the most talented artists, designers and creative professionals on earth. We collectively help each other develop our careers and push our agendas forward. We also create and manage our own brands either as independent properties or direct assets of the KDU and consult other brands on a variety of brand-building services, from creative direction and design to finance, legal, licensing and business acceleration services.

▲▼ KDU graphics

Founded by: **Paul Budnitz**
When: **2002**
Where: **Los Angeles, USA**
Website: **www.kidrobot.com**

One aspect of streetwear that is often missed by those who are not familiar with the subculture, is that clothing, for the majority of the designers and artists involved, represents another medium through which they can express themselves. The majority of streetwear designers do not consider themselves to be fashion designers, but artists. The majority of the artists Kidrobot work with are also part of the larger street culture phenomena. The urban vinyl toy phenomena started in 1997 when toy designer Michael Lau presented his first customized GI Joe toys, which he had 'dressed' to resemble hip hop figures. Ever since, a million-dollar business has emerged that produces original and limited collectible art in the form of toys for adults. Paul Budnitz was so enthralled by the vinyl toy scene and its artistic potential that he set

◀ Dunny series

▲ Shuttlemax by Mill McMullen

▲ Ganesh by Doze Green

up Kidrobot in 2001. It has since grown to be the market leader, collaborating with many highly talented artists. It has also opened three stores in San Francisco, Los Angeles and New York. Kidrobot has also just launched a clothing line to accompany their incredible artist output.

What does streetwear mean to you, from a personal and a business point of view?

Streetwear is a form of pop art, and of folk art. So certain designs are created, almost indigenously, by people and those designs begin to permeate fashion, design and toys.

How did you get involved in streetwear, and when?

I've always been involved. In the late 1980s I had a clothing company with a friend. We made giant silk-screens and covered clothing in ink. In the 1990s I had a company that modified vintage clothing, and sold it to the Japanese and in Europe. Now it's Kidrobot. It's all connected.

Where do streetwear's strengths and weaknesses lie?

The group mind is alchemical, meaning: things that are invented spontaneously by a group of people are very interesting and very strong because all these people are inventing something, and the result is bigger than the parts.

That's why street art, folk art and pop art are so powerful. It's magic in a way. The only issue is that some things can be trendy, and come and go before they have had time to really develop.

Where is streetwear going?
I have no idea. I try not to know. That would ruin everything.

Where do you want to take Kidrobot?
We've been doing toys for almost four years now, and we're moving into clothing and animation this year. Plus we're publishing a book on toys and I've designed part of Peter Gatien's new nightclub in Toronto. I'm hoping someone will ask me to design a car someday!

What were the most memorable events that had an impact on you, and on streetwear?
For me it's personal moments, like when I realized that collaboration is, in itself, an art form, and I decided to make my business about people working together, not alone. That led us to really involving our customers in our art

form (we encourage our fans and message board members to comment on toy designs, even to make those designs). So that realization was about inclusion. I heard Bob Dylan quoted as saying 'Nostalgia is Death', which clarified my position that Kidrobot only looks forward, never backwards. I don't watch TV or read magazines much so I'm not really big on 'cultural' moments. I just don't find those things real.

The key to success in business, is longevity. How do you see this, and how do you apply it to your design work and business development/practice?
We have so many characters, we invent so much stuff. We're not just a logo or a label, we're something real. Our philosophy has always been that everything we do must

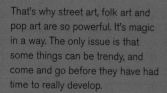

◀ Monger series

be undeniable. And we have to be totally open and transparent to our customers, to have real integrity in how we do business. So if we do that, I don't think there's actually anything more we CAN do. It's up to our customers and fans to tell us if we're doing a good job. I love the work we do, so in a way I'm one of them.

choosing to like something edgy, without being too cool or stiff about it, they can be themselves and include everyone. I just love the toys, and the clothing, the bright colours, the edginess, the risk of it. It is just so joyful.

What do you love about streetwear?

Its openness and inclusiveness, the fact that the customers know me, the fans know the artists, and the fans ARE the artists, and everyone connects and works together. We're really working for a culture of openness and of people being together, and that is our strength. We're never snobby, even though our stuff is limited edition and exclusive in a way. So our customers can be heroic, by

Picture credits:
Flowbots by JK5-kidrobot6
Dunny Series 3-kidrobot5
Shuttlemax by Bill McMullin-kidrobot2
Kidrobot 11 by Kidrobot-kidrobot3
Mongers by Frank Kozik-kidrobot4
Ganesh by Doze Green-kidrobot1

▶ Kidrobot 11 by Kidrobot

KNOW1EDGE

Founded by: **Julius Brian Siswojo**   When: **1999**   Where: **Hong Kong, China**   Website: **www.know1edge.com**

Know1edge was established by Julius Brian, following his involvement in the Hong Kong skate scene. In 1999, he set up a distribution company selling his favourite skateboard brands and went on to open a shop, named after his business postcode, 8FIVE2. Brian has since become a skateboarding ambassador and represents Hong Kong street culture to the outside world. It was from this distribution and retail experience that Brian's own brand Know1edge emerged.

What does streetwear mean to you, from a personal and business point of view?

Streetwear is a part of a lifestyle with a unique and creative history. Nowadays it includes many varieties from different influences so it's more how you wear clothing than a set style, but the lifestyle is the same. From a business point of view, it's hard to think of streetwear because everyone I know has become or have been friends of mine. There are times when it's frustrating as a distributor: where do I go with a brand that I think is dope that should be supported even though it isn't selling well? Sometimes people are late to see this, but this is also the appeal of streetwear: it's dope, super limited, rare and fresh.

How did you get involved in streetwear, and when/where?

Again, it sounds clichéd but 'Skateboarding Saved My Life'! I started in 1986 in Hong Kong. Everything else just followed. To this day, life is all about skateboarding, family, eating, living, working, breathing and being with wifey.

Where do streetwear's strengths and weaknesses lie?

It's definitely the many talented people! Wherever you go in the world there is an unsaid bond between anyone in the skate community and streetwear culture and for the most part everyone I've met have been really good people. The weaknesses? It's not a wealthy culture with a lot of financial support so there are many things you just can't do. Sometimes, people hate a brand and then go out and work with them on a collaboration the next day because they're just trying to survive. Or when a larger corporation tries to bank on what they think can profit instead of supporting the scene the proper way. I understand they just have to go with it because it's the only way they know how to survive.

Where is streetwear going?

Scary to say; corporate people are always looking for something lucrative and they know that streetwear/lifestyle is where the money's at in the near future.

◀ Brian with white t-shirt and 8FIVE2 hat, photo by Tabo

Corporate heads are buying out all these brands. Of course, many of us need the money for several reasons so they will sell the company and unless the same talented people are running the company, it'll go down for sure! You can't front, you got to know what you're doing and customers are pickier now. They can feel that inconsistency in the designs they've been supporting.

Which memorable events had an impact on you, and on streetwear?

I consider myself blessed to live in Hong Kong where so many talented OG heads pass through so often. Just meeting so many smart, gifted people has made an impact on the culture in Hong Kong. Among those I have to really thank is Alyasha Owerka-Moore. He introduced me to many of the people I know today.

I met him by chance one day at the local skate spot. His belief in my vision was one of the reasons I got started in all of this.

The key to success in business is longevity. How do you see this and how do you apply it to your business development and practice, and design work?

Working in the fast-paced lifestyle of Hong Kong, I know the importance of constantly growing and being willing to relearn and improve. Know1edge is about a higher learning in life. I'm always thinking of new ways to improve things. My goal is to improve the quality of Know1edge, maintain affordability and stay consistent with our designs. 8FIVE2shop and 8FIVE2Distribution is now into its eighth year but we are only just starting to be known. Many

people start shops these days and wonder within the first six months why their business isn't doing as well as they hoped. Well, many people don't know that I started my shop out of my apartment that I shared with my three siblings, mother and father. There were many years when it seemed more of a struggle than anything profitable, but I stood by my belief that one day it would get better. Old-fashioned diligence and hard work is the key to success in longevity, but I'll let you know in another ten years. The most important thing now is to really choose the right people that I want to work with to develop it properly. You just can't do it all by yourself.

What are the differences and similarities of streetwear in Hong Kong compared to the rest of the world?

▶ Brian and Annie in the studio, photo by Pak Khei (Studio8)

▲ Brian, photo by Annie Lee

Streetwear in Hong Kong has definitely developed over the last five years. Back in the days, it was so different. They wore double polo shirts in two different colours, super bell-bottom jeans called York, Dr Marten fo sho, and everyone was rocking Bold Bag or Mandarina Duck. I used to rock Dr Marten eight-hole burgundy boots but the problem wasn't about what they wore but how they pieced everything together with no sense of personal style. We've come a long way since those days. Now ninety-eight per cent of the teenagers here wear their jeans a little lower on the waist. It's definitely a different culture. Hong Kong's scene has been into high-end fashion for a long time. They started to wear streetwear clothing about seven years ago. It seems in the last year or so, Hong Kong's street fashion has come close to the leaders (New York and Tokyo). The good thing about Hong Kong is that people are willing to try new things and constantly search for what's the newest. The downfall would definitely be that they still feel awkward wearing the clothing. It could be a confidence issue and again that would stem from the Asian family upbringing.

Why did you start Know1edge and where do you want to go with it?
I started Know1edge with selfish intentions. I wanted a brand where every aspect of the line appealed to me, where I could get artists that I really respected to collaborate on different projects that they normally would not do. I just want to make nice, simple, good quality clothing, maintain its affordability with attention to details to those that appreciate it and continue working with amazing people.

MARRIED TO THE MOB

Girls have often been overlooked by the streetwear subculture. So Married to the Mob started off as a duo of highly motivated women from New York who aimed to provide streetwear at the same level of quality that other leading brands of the genre have been doing over the past ten years for men. Married to the Mob has since morphed into a tribe of like-minded ladies from all over the world, spearheaded by Leah McSweeney, the original founder of the brand. Included below are a few excerpts from their blog, an online diary of what it is like to live the Married to the Mob lifestyle.

Founded by: **Leah McSweeney**
When: **2004**
Where: **New York, USA**
Website: **www.marriedtothemobnyc.com**

THIRTY DAYS AND GOING
STRONG…
posted by tab on March 31
at 7:07 am

This is being written by Leah btw.
Wow thirty fucking days today.
I haven't had a sip of booze or any
drugs for that matter either. Not
like I fucked with drugs that much.
I went through my hardcore drug
phase at a much younger age.
I was over it by age 20 after
spending most of my adolescence
tweeked out. I had done the
complete sober thing once for six
months in 2001 from March–Aug/
Sept. but things were crazed back
then. This month has been amazing.
I think I have gotten more done this
month than out of any month in my
entire life. And as most of you know
I am a real fucking booze head.

I mean a serious lush. I've had
broken teeth, numerous bar/
restaurant/lounge/club brawls,
too many black outs and even
fights with celebrities. It's such a
trip living life without any mind-
altering anything. I'm kind of high
all the time. I definitely feel kind of
weird, like I never turn off. I have
a lot of problems getting to sleep
at night. But I can't complain. My
boyfriend has nothing to yell at me
about, my mom is totally rooting
for me and all my friends are being
mad supportive. But hey, I have lil
Tab and Sweet 16 to set a good
example for. And how can I yell at
them for stupid shit when I am doing
all the stupid shit myself? I will see
how long my sobriety lasts but my
goal is not to drink until I am on my
Wallypower 118 in the middle of the
Mediterranean. And then I will have

a much-deserved glass of Moët
with chambord. Yum!

BITCHES LISTEN UP … STOP
FIGHTING LIKE BITCHES!!
posted by leah on April 7 at 7:35 am

Holy Fuck. When it comes to
fighting, girls are way dirtier than
dudes. We grab hair and don't let go,
we gang up, we pull out piercings
and we spit and throw drinks in
faces. I personally fight like a guy.
But I come from a family of great
fighters (boxers that is). I have never
fought like a bitch. And listen, I don't
want anyone getting the wrong
idea. I don't go out and start fights
for fun like a total asshole. But if
the situation arises I don't mind
throwing down if I'm in the right
mood (or wrong mood).

▲ Spend Hard t-shirt
▼ Wu/Mob collaboration t-shirt

▲ Spend Hard t-shirt
▼ Men are the new women sticker

▲ Spend Hard t-shirt
▼ Wu/Mob collaboration t-shirt

▲ Story t-shirt
▼ Story t-shirt

And how 'bout Vanessa the Molesta. Our
21 years! And we are only 23. That is sisterhood
the most gangsta girl I have ever met. She's done
fck out of a car and sold white to Saudi
n their 20 million dollar townhouses. She even threw
my ass when I was about to get jumped by some
princes. We can't forget Downtown Emily Brown.
and sweet voice too. You've probably
whether it be in a magazine, on a billboard in
n nightclub wilding. She flew in Miami in route to
home's on her way to big things.

First off hair pulling is a straight-up bitch move. Pulling on jewelry and piercings also another bitch move. A real fight should consist of a smack followed by a punch followed by a headlock and so forth. Ladies, you know who you are, why do you all fight like silly-ass hoes? Get some fucking technique and some class! That's right I said class. And learn how to throw a fucking punch! Another thing that's fucked up is ganging up. It should be fair, one on one. Luckily the one time I had two girls fighting me, at the sports bar in Chelsea, the neighbourhood pimp had my back and smacked one of those bitches and told me to run. As I ran I threw an empty bottle of Cristal in their direction. Throwing a bottle in someone's direction is ok. But breaking a bottle over someone's head is not cool!

Unless they did some fucked-up shit!! Like it's your best friend and she fucked your boyfriend or some nasty shit like that.

Fighting should be a last resort. Just know that the majority of females don't want to brawl. They might talk shit but can't back it up. The minute you turn around and say something snappy back to someone after they talk some shit to you they get shook. That's why you should always be ready to get it on if you want to talk shit. You just might talk some shit to the wrong girl.

JUST ANOTHER NIGHT…
posted by leah on April 18
at 5:52 pm

After drinking the entire bottle of Jim Beam and taking half of the mushrooms the night began. Me and the crew left my apartment with our bag of tricks, we got into a cab making our way across town to a loft party. Upon entering the party we realized something … we left the bag in the cab. Luckily Pakistani people are really sweet and our cab driver came back to give us our lost items. You see why I'm trying to do the sober thing?!

◀ Money t-shirt

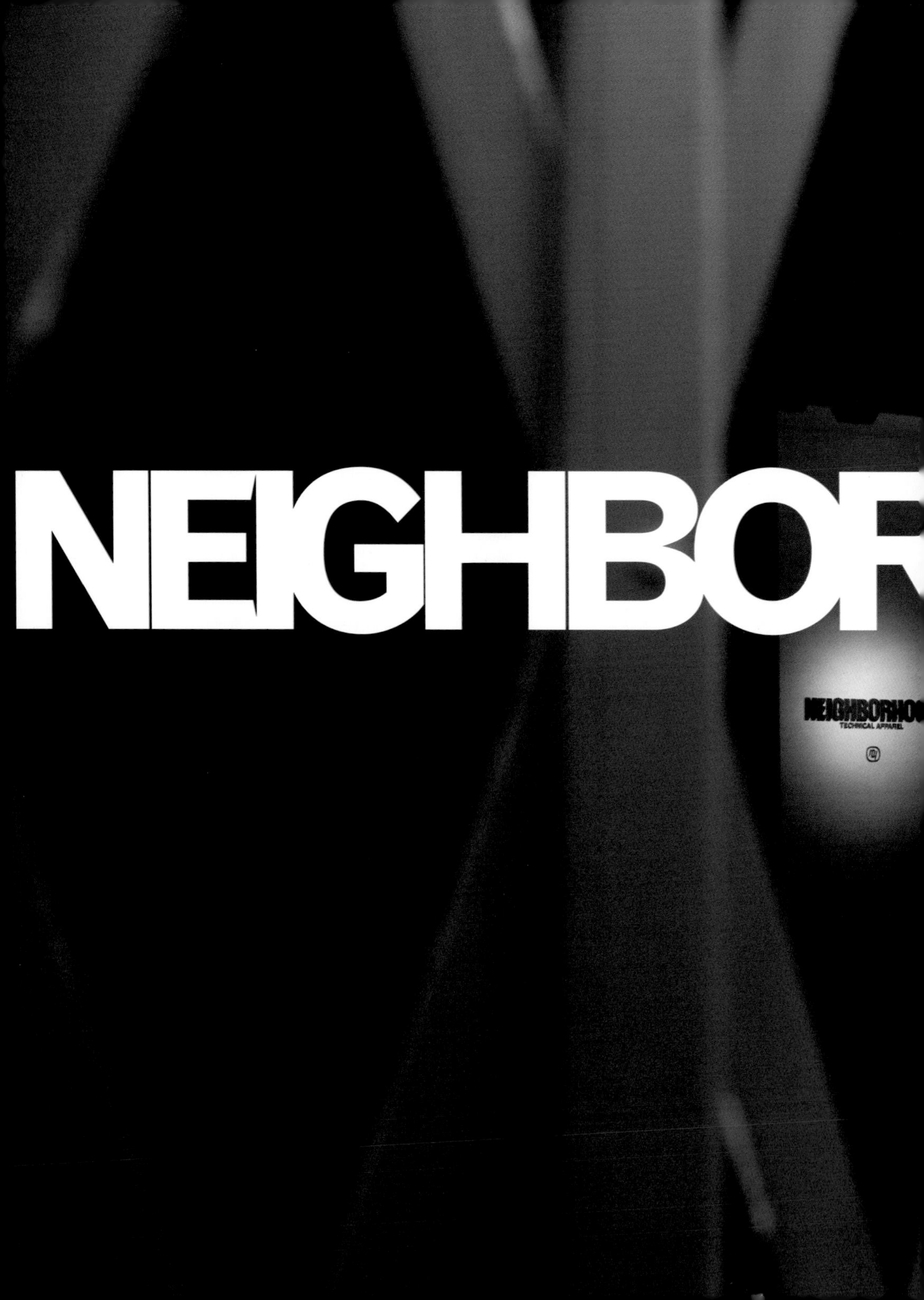
NEIGHBOR
TECHNICAL APPAREL

HOOD

Founded by: **Shinsuke Takizawa**
When: **1994**
Where: **Tokyo, Japan**
Blog: **http://blog.honeyee.com/stakizawa**

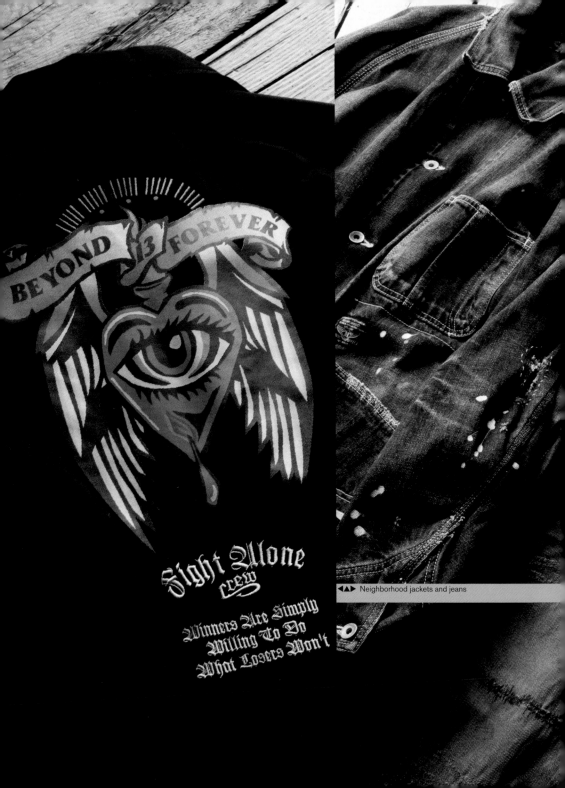

BEYOND 13 FOREVER

Fight Alone
crew

Winners Are Simply
Willing To Do
What Losers Won't

◀▲▶ Neighborhood jackets and jeans

NEIGHBORHOOD was founded by Shinsuke Takizawa in 1994 with a simple premise in mind – one that they've managed to hold on to as the brand has grown – he wanted to create basic, usable, but very desirable clothing inspired by the kind of rugged apparel typically worn by the military or found in motorcycle culture. NEIGHBORHOOD was conceived as a retail experience as well as a brand, and in the same year that the brand was launched, Shinsuke opened a store on Cat Street in the Harajuku district of Tokyo – the very heart of Japanese street culture.

After four years of success, NEIGHBORHOOD moved to larger premises in Harajuku and started presenting his new collections twice a year, typically at streetwear exhibitions. Now, some twelve years after Shinsuke founded the brand, in addition to their Tokyo store in Harajuku, NEIGHBORHOOD has been expanded further, by distributing to stores such as 'Blackflag', the select Tokyo store that they opened in 2005, a branch of NEIGHBORHOOD in Osaka, five 'HOODS' stores in Japan, and streetwear throughout both Japan and the rest of the world.

Today, a NEIGHBORHOOD collection still contains the elements of what originally inspired Shinsuke to start the brand – high-quality, vintage-feel denims, leather motorcycle jackets from which you can even get a whiff of motorcycle oil, and the accessories they have been collaborating on with Yoshida&Co. They've diversified too, with the brand including products for women, children, babies (and dogs), as well as a range of toys, but irrespective of the areas in which Shinsuke continually experiments and explores, the NEIGHBORHOOD brand has always stayed close to its roots on the streets of Harajuku.

Special thanks to Yass Endo and Akiko Shiraishi

◀ A selection of products and inspiration

▲▶ Jeans, jacket and hat

▲ Jacket
▶ Parka

NIKE
(FRASER COOKE)

Founded by: **Philip Knight & Bill Bowerman**
When: **1972**
Where: **Beaverton, USA**
Website: **www.nike.com**

▲▼ Fraser Cooke

Fraser Cooke's official job is Global Urban Marketing Director for Nike. It's a pretty non-descriptive job title, but in very basic terms, it means that Fraser is Nike's man, worldwide, connecting the machinery that is Nike with the international elite of the street culture world.

Prior to joining Nike, Fraser worked with Michael Kopelman in London on some of the most important and forward-thinking projects in streetwear and sneaker culture, such as The Hit and Run shop, now called the Hideout, as well as running the Foot Patrol shop

in Soho. His influence on the streetwear culture is felt around the world, and has done so for longer than most people have been involved in the industry. Currently residing in Tokyo, Fraser offers us an insight into what he thinks about this subculture.

What does the term streetwear mean to you?

Streetwear basically means a culture or series of movements that emanate from the ground up. They are born in the streets, usually springing from the young and less financially advantaged, and mostly involve a musical element, style of dress associated, perhaps a visual imagery that binds it together and often a drug. Mod, punk, hip hop, skate etc. These movements are usually the result of bored youth getting creative and inspired, doing it for themselves and growing something organically.

How did you get involved in streetwear and when?

Through skateboarding initially, which hit the UK in the summer of 1977. There was also the punk thing exploding at a similar time. I was a bit young for that, but I remember the Sex Pistols on the Bill Grundy show and the energy and shock that was being created. The UK was, and still is, a very fertile place for these subcultures to grow. I was lucky to grow up in the suburbs of London and be close to, and participate in, some great moments in youth culture history, before it became as scrutinized and subsequently capitalized upon as it is today. Now there is little time for any incubation of a scene and that is key to its development.

Where do streetwear's strengths and weaknesses lie?

Its strengths are in its ability to come up with fast-moving changes or left-field ideas that move faster than anyone could predict or plan for. When that happens it's amazing. I think that for any generation, especially if you are experiencing things for the first time and are in your teens and twenties, it offers a healthy creative channel for kids to get involved in and make friendships that can last for years. Music, graphics, painting, clothing design — these are all great things for younger people to express themselves through. And for others who just want to be around it, streetwear offers an escape from the mundane normality of everyday life. It allows people to dream. I think the only weaknesses I see are just a manifestation of its track record of success and the shift in the way that media works today. These things have conspired to change behaviour. The spotlight is always searching for something new in order for hordes of people to justify their jobs that rely on reporting, or selling to this audience, which is now huge due to instantaneousness, and to the global nature of the web today. Magazines are less relevant now but did play a part throughout the 1990s until a few years ago. There is far more exposure of street culture to more people than ever before and you don't have to live in London, New York or Tokyo to be a part of it. You don't really even need to go there, although I think that those who travel and make real human connections are better able to create a more thorough end result than those who just experience it through a computer screen. But there is a great deal of repetition. Many people are buying into street culture products without having any idea why they are doing it, other than knowing it's cool. Learn about why these things exist and take an interest in pushing it forward. There is too much passive consumerism.

Where is streetwear going?

At the moment it seems to be growing but not reinventing itself enough. In some untapped places, as things spread across the globe to people who had no access to street culture, such as China, India or parts of South America.

◀ Left to right: Eddie Cruz, Aaron Rose & Fraser Cooke

You see a bigger audience and more participants in what have become known as key elements of street culture: mostly hip hop, skate, graffiti and punk. Within that new audience, scenes are growing and cool things are inevitably created that add to the culture as a whole. There's also a lot more crap to filter through and that is the main negative side. Sometimes the blind are leading the blind. We are in an era of remix: everything on almost every level is 'sampled' from the past. That's why so many influential people exist who were a part of the original generation that created many of these movements. They have the 'beats' to sample from, to use a hip hop analogy. There is less distinction between my generation and the ones that came afterwards. They are still rehashing the same ideas. I would like to see more original ideas and new unexpected movements. When I saw *Rize* by David LaChapelle, I thought, wow, where the hell did that come from? It was a scene that was going on undetected. Grime in the UK was refreshing a few years ago. I don't love the sound but it's got energy and attitude and if I was sixteen, I know I'd be into it. It has an edge.

Which memorable events had an impact on you and in turn, on streetwear?

The advent of punk, the amazing creativity of the skate and hip hop movements. A few actual moments for me were seeing the Buffalo Gals video by Malcolm McClaren for the first time or seeing the Dogtown crew skate a pool on TV back in the late 1970s. Both were like witnessing something from outer space. Later on, seeing Shawn Stüssy, and the tribe that he surrounded himself with, fuse these cultures together, in which, we were by now participating in. A fresh way with his So Cal surf aesthetics through the early Stüssy ads in *Thrasher* magazine. He invented streetwear in its current form, that's for sure.

What do you love about this culture?

The fact that I and many others can continue to be inspired by our peers and young up-and-comers and that it's an alternative outlet for creativity for so many and it's growing. The great friends that I've made through the years all over the world and the experiences both then and to come.

OBEY

Founded by: **Shepard Fairey**   When: **1989**   Where: **Los Angeles, USA**   Website: **www.obeygiant.com**

Shepard Fairey started his multi-media assault on the senses in 1989. But not content with setting up in towns all over America, Shepard began printing his designs onto clothing (t-shirts in particular), causing the Obey brand to explode into a wordwide phenomenon. These t-shirts (and later his entire collection) became just another medium onto which he could project his message and ideas, which are often political, ranging from critical appropriations of current political situations to using Soviet-style propaganda colour schemes.

Music also plays a large part of the Obey campaign, including hip hop and punk. It comes as no surprise that Shepard's work now incorporates all things street related, be it toys, CD covers and guitar designs, events or parties. He also produces his own magazine *Swindle*, makes stickers, has written several books and even produces his own CDs.

Regardless of his many and varied activities, Shepard has never forgotten his roots and still goes out painting at night to spread the message.

What does the term streetwear mean to you?

Streetwear is a broad term. It is basically clothing that comes out of the urban culture which is heavily influenced by and influences punk, hip hop, graffiti and clubbing. Streetwear is much more populist than fashion, it has a very strong do-it-yourself mentality and is very avant-garde, in the sense that it doesn't follow the obvious design cycles of fashion. One point, in my opinion, that does get confused quite often is that even though all of the participants in streetwear, or in the street culture, have a skateboarding background, streetwear does not equal skatewear. Stüssy is a good example of that. I also think that streetwear has a certain level of pride attached to it, unlike fashion, since it is made for individuals, and people with the same ideals as you. The problem that I see with streetwear now, though, is that too many people have jumped on the streetwear bandwagon and are strangling the creative output with tons of products which do not reflect the true spirit of streetwear. It is saturated at the moment.

How did you get involved in streetwear?

I have always been very active in the skate, punk and political hip hop scene and through what I was doing with Obey and my graffiti work, I really wanted to add my two cents and spread my message with the rest of them.

Back then, you could walk down the street and if you saw somebody wearing a skate or punk band t-shirt, you were bound to have something, if not a lot, in common with them. That's why I thought it would be a really good idea to expand into printing my designs onto t-shirts and clothing, because it would just be another medium for my art and for my message. It was exciting to see who would then buy the t-shirts and wear them. I first started making my t-shirts around 1989, at the same time as I started to make stickers. Initially, I just made t-shirts for my friends, and I had no real personal conflict about being considered a sellout by the rest of the graffiti community.

For me they were exactly the same thing in principle. I think it was then that I realized that it was actually easier to be an artist than running a company that produced and sold clothing.

All of a sudden, rip-off t-shirts appeared with my designs on them in stores like Urban Outfitters. I just came to a point where I needed to take Obey clothing more seriously as a brand in order to have control over my own image.

▲ Heavy Metal Parking Lot cap

▲ Chest Ink (Raglan)

▲ Portfolio Jacket

▲ London Dungeon Stripe Knit

▲ Repeat poster t-shirt

▲ Boss Man blazer

▲ Back Up woven shirt

▲ Top Gunner t-shirt

▲ Scritti Politti cap

▲ Whiskey jacket   ▲ Muslim Girl t-shirt   ▲ Pin Head sweater

▲ Street Sweeper jacket   ▲ Rouge cap   ▲ Metal Head t-shirt

▲ Molotov t-shirt   ▲ No Scene sweater   ▲ High Time cap

Music always plays a big part in your imagery. How has it influenced your work in particular?

Music, and especially punk rock music, really changed my life. I was your typical frustrated teenager, and punk rock and skateboarding really opened my eyes. It meant independence and gave me a lot of freedom. I know it's a cliché nowadays, and I have even seen people telling this story because they think it's their way into this whole scene and subculture, but that really is how it was for me. The whole punk scene, as well as the skateboarding world, had a real do-it-yourself approach which appealed to me. I can remember how when Black Flag started, they had to organize their entire tours by themselves because there was no touring circle for punk bands at the time. Up until then, punk bands were forced to stay in their home towns precisely for that reason. It is exactly that mentality which began to influence me and which eventually encouraged me to set up Obey. Being resourceful and independent is essential.

ONE TRUE SAXON

Founded by: **Ian Pailey**
When: **1999**
Where: **Nottingham, UK**
Website: **www.goodnorth.com**

One of streetwear's most redeeming features is its reluctance to be defined. There are many different facets to this subculture, ranging from technical outerwear to bling-bling all-over prints. ONETrueSaxon, founded by an ordinary bloke who earned his spurs working for Paul Smith, caters for the more serious, older customer. Ian Pailey comes from the north of England, which may be one of the reasons why his approach varies largely from other über-urban brands. Initially, ONETrueSaxon only sold to shops in northern England, but it then went on to conquer the Japanese market. It has a loyal following, and in many respects represents the future of streetwear: ONETrueSaxon's main target group isn't fifteen-year-old skaters, but instead, those who grew up immersed in the streetwear subculture and who now want high-quality clothing and a more subtle design approach. Ian Pailey, former creative director of ONETrueSaxon wrote a short story detailing his thoughts on streetwear:

◀ Masterpiece jeans

▲ Strider jeans vintage wash

▲ Navy marsh parka

▲ Cats and dogs jacket

Graduation.

The definition of streetwear is what is worn on the street. I guess it depends what streets are like where you grow up. Whether it is music street, football street, hip hop street or just plain nasty street. Add a 'z' onto the end of all words to give authenticity. I guess 'k' also works. Looking at it logically, all of the real playerz (sic) in the scene are hovering either side of their mid-thirties, and therefore draw a massive influence from the late 1980s schoolin' style when BBC melted into frantic coin-op into ZX. Nicking VW badges, John Craven's outrage at the Beasties, Taggin' with school pens. These are the constant threads that keep the scene retro. Not helped by the u-turn from the early 1990s of the major sports houses deciding that looking back is good way of stalling the new ideas fund. These are all nods to the wise for the drivers of the scene.

These references also remain constant across the cultural genres of street, dance and football. All of which follow the same routine from Birmingham to Berlin. I remember a few key moments, some real playground appreciation from older kids for a genuine fishtail mod parka complete with beer mats and Lambretta patches. I was nine and my brother had given it to me. The same year saw my first kick dilemma, adidas kick or Puma set? Tricky. I went for kick and in hindsight it was the right choice. I did wear them with odd fluorescent socks. So it began, nine years old and wanting to look the part. Aspirations then jumped to a Repro MA-1 in Navy with a custom Black Sabbath patch with the school yard football colours.

The next choice wandered into the accessories world, as equally important to an emerging teenager. The shoe bag, red/grey Nike or fluorescent adidas in orange (much preferable to the lime option). The useless bag, used for everything except what it was designed for. Books didn't fit and pens leaked the second they were put in it.

The generation that schooled in the 1980s is the generation that has the honour of being in charge of street culture: we are now writers, shop keepers, established artists, designers, musicians all with insight and history to make things happen. We are the corporation that encompasses street culture. I wouldn't say that the members of this 'corporation' are necessarily cutting-edge. This is left to the new street, the new graduates from late 1990s schoolin', all starting up in business looking over their shoulders at the next lot emerging.

The faces of the corporation, the original graduates, are the new wave of industry, the consultants to the last wave, the final outing of the branded goods gang desperate to reinvent themselves and buy credibility and youth expertise. The corporation does this well, it's the commodity that bankrolls it. I'd put around eight years on a cycle to run before the corporation starts looking for its own consultants.

I'm interested to see what the late 1990s graduates have to offer the UK. It was a period when the dominant culture was ours.

We all grow up and our aspirations and expectations become more luxurious. We demand better quality. There comes a point where street culture gets on a bus you can never buy a ticket for. It's at this point that the potential for influence is at its highest. For a generation where street has been a constant, this leap into adulthood is just too far a jump to make. This is where casualwear driven by a life of street, creeps into the general psyche of the nation.

The back shot of this allows the corporation to inject aspirations of expense and quality back into street culture, and evolving the scene to attract those aged thirty to fifty, the new premium market place where the customer is armed with a black amex. Japan does this extraordinarily well because it infuses random global ideas into domestic products. British street culture is a rich cousin to US mass culture.

Japan remains a key focus for so many: a giant glitter ball constantly reflecting the many different facets of global culture in its own unique rose-tinted way. Its domestic core remaining largely unseen.

▼ Wedmore shoe   ▼ Cumbra shoe

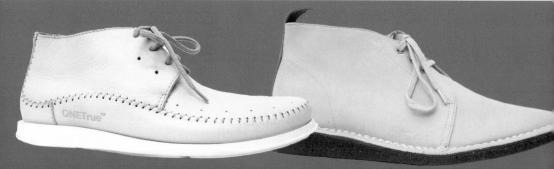

▲ Reproduction batwing jacket

▲ Hooded bonded fleece

PAM

Founded by: **Perks & Mini**
When: **2000**
Where: **Melbourne, Australia**
Website: **www.perksandmini.com**

PAM, also known as Perks and Mini, certainly isn't your average streetwear clothing company. Perks and Mini embody the constant discussion within the streetwear industry to the fullest, since they are not just an average fashion company that churns out collection after collection. PAM consists of the creative team Shaun and Misha, who create books, movies, toys, artwork, art installations and clothing lines. PAM was set up in Australia, but this geographical isolation has not had an adverse impact on their contribution to the subculture. Misha talks here about what streetwear means to him and PAM.

How do you define streetwear?
Streetwear is really easy to define: comfortable clothing. This is the most important 'rule' of streetwear, and not just comfortable in the

▲ Autumn/Winter 06/07 Peace and Menace

physical sense. Streetwear is relaxed: the philosophy, the construction and the concept. The anti-uptight, the anti-uniform, the anti 'I feel like a dick in these clothes'. This is what sets streetwear apart from other modes of dressing. Stüssy pants were comfortable in the early 1980s. They helped doing bonelesses off cop cars, and hanging out on the couch. They looked cool and fresh, and set a new functional, fashion and lifestyle statement. They were the next step in the formation of what became streetwear, after the t-shirt that is. And sneakers! As a teenager in Burwood, a suburb of Melbourne in Australia, streetwear was exciting. As with the JimmyZ beret and 'off the wall' Vans slip-ons, but also with 'writer jacket' Tuxan shoe paint, PK Ripper BMX, Troma and Phantasm films (and Bones Bridgade!!!), Public Enemy and Suicidal. Later to become Acid house, Shaw Brothers films, smiley faces, LSD, and MA1 flight jackets. Troop and British Knights. Fast forward to now, the elements are still here, but always evolving. And for me, it's about going deeper, but ultimately the same, weird psych from Turkey, art music from Terry Riley and Steve Reich, Czech New Wave cinema, OM flyers

Spring/Summer 06 #1 Wieners

◀ Autumn/Winter 04/05
Lights Over Egypt

▲ Autumn/Winter 04/05 Lights Over Egypt   ▲ Autumn/Winter 04/05 Lights Over Egypt

(SE racing's aptly named 'OLD MAN' 26" Cruiser), German cars, and German 'kraut' rock, Claes Oldenburg, DADA, handmade shoes, and the search for the next level of t-shirt graphic. Streetwear to me is popular culture. It's also a reflection of new and fresh ideas. To be honest, streetwear in its current state has become boring and repetitious. A new colour way for dunks, BIG DEAL!!! Dunks to begin with, whatever!!!! Collaborations with popular ideas from the past, boring!!!! (But good for business.) Streetwear, best represented by t-shirt graphics, should move forward, not linger around the golden years of early hip hop. Experimentation is what makes for a better and more interesting product. Of course this is much more difficult, and more of a 'business' risk, but ultimately more exciting and truer to the philosophy and spirit of where it all comes from: punk in all its forms, the youth, the fuckups, free thinkers, skateboarders (and surfers), graffiti writers and fresh kids. Streetwear is about all this. It is a 'fuck you' free-spiritness, which is not about blogs and staleness. It's about standing up and showing the world that you don't give a fuck what THEY think! The t-shirt, and the sag in your pants, and undone shoelaces are all a symbol of this.

POINTER

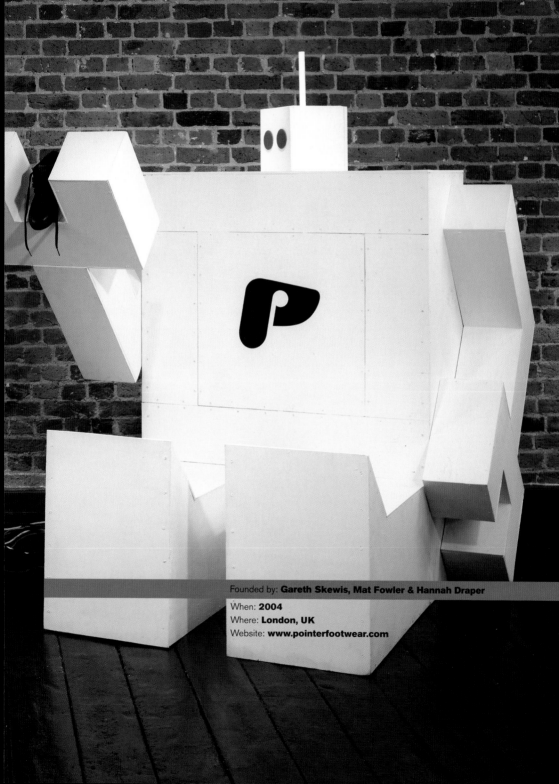

Founded by: **Gareth Skewis, Mat Fowler & Hannah Draper**

When: **2004**
Where: **London, UK**
Website: **www.pointerfootwear.com**

Footwear company Pointer was founded in 2004 to offer an alternative to technical sneakers and bulky skateboarding shoes. Knowing its streetwear-inspired shoes would suit a niche market rather than competing with major footwear companies, Pointer set out to produce classic, casual and comfortable footwear with low-key designs. Founder Gareth Skewis discusses streetwear in the following essay.

Streetwear – a rant from the inside.

Streetwear. What a vague combination of words. I don't remember when the clothes I wore got that label. But I do remember skating down the street on a brand new Real Tommy G, shaved head, Dead Kennedy's T, white three-stripe gym socks up to my knees and a pair of black three-hole Dr Martens. My mom had just got me the board from Slam City Skates on a trip to the UK; my gran sent me the shirt after I begged her for months to brave the then-shitty shops on Carnaby Street. The shorts: wearing camouflage if you were a civilian was illegal in South Africa until 1993, as I soon found out from being busted skating by a cop in riot gear. And the shoes? They were my chilling shoes; for

skating, I usually rocked Converse All Stars held together with duct tape, or Vans Full Cabs if I could get them.

I had the best route from my house to the local shop – although there was a group of French Nazi Skin kids living on the corner who took great joy in calling me a yank-loving, black-loving little shit. Before I left Johannesburg I could count on running into a few of these fine gentlemen every week … but that's another story, and I don't think people who are into clothing and shoes would be very interested in that. Anyway: I had styled myself on Mat Hensley meets Minor Threat meets Andy Howell, although all I was really listening to at the time was De La Soul, Bodycount and Bad Brains. I was a part of a small but growing white youth culture in Johannesburg who had found an alternative to rugby, beer, pulling your trousers up too high and generally kicking people's asses on Friday nights. Instead I was obsessed with Dinosaur Jr, Airwalk shoes, Blind Video Days, Sonic Youth, Chris Hall, Southbank, The Smiths, Pushead, Eightball clothing, Black Flag, Danny Way, Warhol, the ANC, the Circle Jerks, SST records, Death Box and the Clash.

The late 1980s and early 1990s was an odd time in South Africa.

Thanks to the ever-charming Apartheid government, it was almost impossible to get hold of anything of interest: new music took months to arrive, and international magazines like *NME*, *Thrasher*, *Transworld*, *RAD* and *Rolling Stone* were about a year old by the time that they got to us. So we were left in the dark, and to our own devices. The first time I heard Nirvana I was convinced that they would all look like Suicide or the Pixies. It was six months later when, on a trip to Brazil, I saw Smells Like Teen Spirit on MTV and knew what grunge looked like.

So what does this all have to do with a London shoe company? Growing up in South Africa gave me the chance not to be biased by what was perceived as super cool or super lame. No one to say: 'That red Stüssy hat you've been wearing for a year is so last season'. I was forced to have an opinion.

And now I wonder: how did we get to a point where product is no longer king, and hype rules us like a middle-aged gym teacher? 'Get up that rope, boy; who do you think you are?' became 'White Pantone leather is going to be huge this season: you should design an entire line out of it'. Give me a bloody break; that stuff is disgusting. I grew up believing that streetwear

was anti-fashion, was about creating your own independent and unique scene, not bending over to be in with the cool kids — and certainly not lead by marketing and hype. Where did all the individual senses go? Across the globe, kids are consuming the same big brands.

In streetwear, as with most other self-obsessed and highly critical trends, those not concerned with becoming the next big thing or the latest cool kid on the block seem to become that without trying. People who don't give a damn what you, me, the CEO of the VF Corp, some kid queuing for a hat in Tokyo, or supercoolkidsblog. com think. Pointer has always been about having our own scene and working with people who we respect, appreciate, and, most importantly, are our friends. That is what the next few pages of artwork are about: giving friends freedom to be creative under a common brand. Not, let's get so-and-so because his limited t-shirt for such-and-such corp smashed it in Japan this week. Bloody good for him, but personally I don't really give a damn. Surely streetwear can still be about being open-minded and having the right to be into whatever you want … or maybe I have it completely wrong?

◀ Pointer graphics

▶ Growler

THE QUIET LIFE

Founded by: **Andy Mueller**
When: **1997**
Where: **California, USA**
Websites: **www.thequietlife.com**
www.ohiogirl.com
www.lakai.com
www.theartdump.com

Andy Mueller was raised in the mid-west on a healthy diet of skateboarding, music, magazines and BMX, and has since been responsible for creating some of the most poignant, understated and well-recognized graphics in skateboarding and streetwear for almost ten years. He runs his own design studio, Ohio Girl, out of which he runs his own clothing label, The Quiet Life, and is also the Art Director for the seminal skateboarding brand, Lakai Footwear. In addition, he belongs to the group of creatives known as The Art Dump. It is within this constellation that he designs new deck graphics for Girl and Chocolate Skateboards and shoots photos for Fourstar, Ruby and the other brands within the Girl/Chocolate family.

▲ Army hoodie
▼ Scribble t-shirt

▲ Camer Club track jacket
▼ Black sweatshirt

▲ Quiet Life logo t-shirt

▲ Bling t-shirt

▲ Bling t-shirt

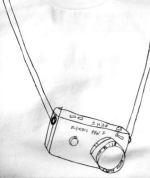

▲ Camera t-shirt

▲ Papercut t-shirt

▲ Camera dot t-shirt

▲ Quiet Life logo t-shirt
▼ I wish I spoke French t-shirt

▲ Cubed logo t-shirt
▼ Paint t-shirt

▲ Teenage Runaway t-shirt
▼ Mid-West t-shirt

I WISH I SPOKE FRENCH

▲ Papercut t-shirt

▲ Love Art t-shirt

▲ Ping Pong t-shirt

▲ Pencil logo t-shirt

▲ Papercut t-shirt

▲ Here comes the future t-shirt

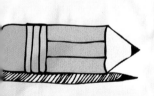

▲ Pencil t-shirt
▼ Pencil pocket t-shirt

▲ Moustache t-shirt
▼ VS t-shirt

▲ Point & Shoot t-shirt
▼ Smoking S t-shirt

▲ Assorted accessories

How would you define streetwear and in what ways has it influenced you over the years?

I'm not really sure what I think about streetwear. I guess I feel kind of funny being asked about it because I never know what to say. I think this is because I don't really think about it or consider myself as part of the 'streetwear' movement or anything like that. I sort of feel like an outsider. To me, I'm just a guy who has been making artwork, doing graphics, and taking photos for a long time, before all the hype. I got involved with doing clothing graphics way back in 1986 when I first learned how to silkscreen and I've been at it ever since. It's just one of the things that I do,

it is part of me. I started working professionally in 1993 when I set up a small design studio called Ohio Girl.

I was mainly doing graphics and photography for bands. This included a lot of band t-shirts. I started working for snowboard companies and that's when things really started to take off. In 1997 I started The Quiet Life project as an internal project through Ohio Girl with a few of my Ohio Girl co-workers. I really wanted to do shirts for myself, I was sort of sick of doing designs only for other people, so that's how The Quiet Life got started – out of the desire for total creative control and as a project for us, one without clients.

It's funny thinking back to those early days. I was living in Chicago at the time and was completely unaware that anybody else was doing t-shirts and clothing. I remember seeing an article about Green Lady around the same time and was blown away by them.

I was pretty shocked and inspired that somebody else was out there. In some ways, I still feel removed from the whole thing, I kind of feel like I just do what I do because I love it and don't care about all the hype around that the t-shirt culture and the streetwear scene has received in the past five years or so. I was doing this before the hype and will continue even if the hype goes away. Overall, I think that

▲ True Love Always t-shirt

streetwear and the t-shirt culture is a good thing. I really like how it allows so many artists from all over the world to be involved and see each other's work. I also really like that it's a great, inexpensive way for artists and designers to get their work out there. I often think about t-shirts and clothing as a template – like a black piece of paper or a canvas, it starts blank and then an artist can make it their own.

I'm into that, I like projects that have a template, like a t-shirt, but can be interpreted in a million ways. I really like it when I see a cool shirt that is done in a way that I would have never thought of. I like that streetwear and the t-shirt culture are really up for pushing the limits.

SBTG

Founded by: **Mark Ong** When: **2003** Where: **Singapore** Website: **www.royalefam.com**

Sneaker customization isn't anything new, but over the past twelve months, it has risen to commercial prominence thanks to those sneaker boutiques that have decided to sell artists' efforts. This was a natural progression for those stores who aimed to stay ahead of their competitors by offering something just a little bit different: a true limited edition. Working under the name SBTG, Singaporean designer Mark Ong has rapidly made a name for himself as a sneaker customizer of considerable note. Having collaborated with Tokyo sneaker legends Chapter and Atmos, and Singapore streetwear boutique Ambush, Mark has also exhibited in some of the world's most coveted stores, including Surrender. He is thus generally regarded as one of streetwear's most respected and talented costumiers and designers. Having collaborated with fellow designer Methamphibian, Mark has now moved on from customizing sneakers to officially designing footwear for international super brands like Nike.

What does the term streetwear mean to you, from a personal and a business point of view?

As far as I can remember, it was meant to be a joke, a fun thing or taking the piss out of something corporate that you didn't like. Childhood dreams made serious. Applying your own rebellious angst-ridden voice, vision and lifestyle to a garment that you would like to be represented with. The 1980s can only happen once, where mistakes became classics. Now it is time to make new mistakes. Business is actually about making money.

How, when and where did you get involved in the streetwear culture?

I can remember this scene quite vividly. It was 1989 and I was nine years old. The sunlight reflected against the tarmac car park floor in my neighbourhood Lutheran church and I think it was about 1 or 2 pm if I'm not wrong. We were standing to attention in our navy blue starched boy's brigade uniform. It was drill lesson time. I already had doubts about joining this uniformed group but I went anyway because I enjoyed the company. My feet were hurting. The metal plates from the soles of the drill boots heated up and penetrated to the soles of my feet. I was in a daze

until I heard a very unique rattling noise of something moving. It was the first time I'd heard it: a mix of metal loosely spinning on an axle, urethane wheels. I acquired sight finally; it was a teenager dressed in loud-printed shorts and a cut-up t-shirt. Hi-top basketball-looking shoes with socks up to his shin. It was the coolest thing I had ever seen up until that point. But what shocked me was when he popped an ollie up the curb that was in his way. I was expecting him to jump off and move it up. It was like nothing could stand in his way. This dude was unstoppable. 'What the fuck??!! Can you actually do that? I need to do that too!' A week passed. I spent the whole week in school drawing 'the skater' in my textbooks. I stopped boy's brigade completely. I wanted to be a skater! I obtained for myself an old banana board. I knew it was different. That dude's board was much bigger and it was all black on top. It had sandpaper on it. I spent all my teenage years skateboarding and drawing influences from around it. They were the best moments of my life.

Where do streetwear's strengths and weaknesses lie?

Both strengths and weaknesses lie in the amount of opportunity today.

Especially with the aid of the world wide web. Your audience is the world if you want to make that happen. The market is so open and we are all allowed somehow or other to express ourselves and earn a living and reputation at the same time.

Where do you think streetwear is going?

Hell and heaven.

What memorable events had an impact on you, and on the streetwear culture?

Pressure flips.

Where do you want to take SBTG in the future?

SBTG is a very manual maturing process that came from collecting a dissatisfaction of existing products. One step at a time till saturation is reached. Stop reinterpreting, start creating.

▶ SBTG packaging

▼ SBTG Air Force 1   ▼ SBTG Dunk Lo   ▼ SBTG Dunk Hi

Founded by Ronnie Bonner, The Shadow Conspiracy is a manufacturer of BMX clothing, bike parts and accessories. Over the past three years The Shadow Conspiracy has proved its superiority in design and hardware, and is renowned within the BMX industry for its meticulous attention to detail and novel advertising campaigns.

Founded by: **Ronnie Bonner**
Where: **Orlando, USA**
When: **2002**
Website: **www.theshadowconspiracy.com**

The Journey

My journey is a little different than most because my background is BMX. Although BMX may seem like it has been around forever, the form it is today began in the 1980s when freestyle was born.

In the 1970s, BMX racing and jumping a 2x4 in the front lawn was all there was to it. In the 1980s, freestyle took over. When the industry took a dive in the 1990s, BMX started a new beginning.

I started my first brand in 1986, when I was sixteen. Streetwear culture was in its infancy and household computers had not yet taken hold. Can you imagine no internet? The way people learned about the world was by 'doing' and not 'googling'. I was so intrigued by the idea of expression that learning design, screen printing and sewing consumed my life, not to mention business and business ethics. As I was going through this learning curve, I hustled shirts during high school and by my senior year was travelling overseas. When I realized I could live this dream and see the world, I quit my part-time job and started my journey. That was the last job I ever had.

BMX opened my eyes to a world that I had no idea existed. It was a chain reaction. I would end up in different parts of the world meeting new and interesting people who ate, lived and slept BMX. One of the most amazing chapters in my life was written because of that shiny-ass chrome Mongoose I bought in sixth grade. That purchase was the first and best decision I ever made.

Jumping ahead twenty years, my interest in product design had reached a point where I needed a new outlet. I wanted a project that challenged our team not only with design but also in function. In addition, I dreamt of structuring a solid company to act as a vehicle and support the distribution of new ideas. It's easy to create hype but true substance is something we didn't want to just talk about, we wanted it to be our foundation.

The Shadow Conspiracy was this new outlet and provided the opportunity to apply the knowledge I learned in the apparel industry to product designs for BMX. Everything from the structuring, team, marketing and design all took place under a cloak of secrecy.

The underlying philosophy of progression launched The Shadow Conspiracy into a brand based on innovation but also with a dimension of secrecy. The juxtaposition of these two elements soon revealed a new chapter of my journey.

Around the time I started Shadow, I met Rickey Kim from Evil Monito. Mr Kim was at a point where he could identify and appreciate the direction I had been pushing the brand. The topic of streetwear culture branching into more diverse interests came up often. The retro builds that many of the heads are feeling now are paying homage to the 1980s. It was only natural at fifteen to go to your chicky's house, not wanting to ride your mom's bike. And rockin' the BMX meant destroying curbs on the way. That's where it all started and the amazing thing now is that people are feeling the history of that lifestyle, and retro builds are opening the door for subcultures to see BMX with new eyes, reconnecting people with their past.

The Casual Suspects and all the bike crews are testaments to this movement. In the midst of all this the invisible:man x The Shadow Conspiracy 24" Cruiser project brought the streetwear and BMX worlds together. Up until now, the street attitude was dominated by hip hop fashion. However, as a whole, we are cultivating a culture that is complex. Not all designs and philosophies have to be based around bling, diamonds and excess. More than ever, we are seeking a life with substance, a journey that can only continue through experiences, connectivity and influence. But, when I speak of nice things, don't get me wrong, I also want the fresh new the kicks, t-shirts and denim that cost a month's salary. But I want them to represent a darker side of life. Brands such as invisible:man, Fiberops, Wtaps and Evil Monito are just a few that I feel a connection with. Their range and rawness helps ease the transition between bling and BMX.

As more choices arise and the power of communication strengthens, individual preference will be revolutionized and define the snapshot of the times we live in. This is already happening. Many have said that street culture is a fad! I disagree because it is already morphing into what it wants to be. It's a sign of progression, growth and stability.

There will always be new players and ideas while others become more mainstream. Trends are the feelers of the future. The styles that stick start the Petri dish on which tomorrow's designers grow. Our ability to classify our experiences and encode them symbolically defines our culture.

And now I want to reintroduce you to BMX. It's my lifestyle. So dust your bike off. Head over to you chicky's house and destroy some curbs on the way. I guarantee you will feel what I have been putting down.

SSUR

Founded by: **Ruslan Karablin** When: **1987** Where: **New York, USA** Website: **www.ssurempirestate.com**

▲ SSUR graphic

Ruslan Karablin, better known to the world of art and design as SSUR, has been a constant presence in the New York downtown art scene for almost fifteen years. As an outside artist with no formal training, Karablin drew heavily on sex, politics, and protest to influence the SSUR aesthetic. Part counterculture, part pop culture and one hundred per cent fun, SSUR presents a truly unique perspective on the world. SSUR runs a store in New York, which sells the regular lines as well as the many special collaborations Karablin has worked on. Rather than submitting to an interview, Ruslan outlines his background and the development of SSUR:

Where I was born and where and how I have lived is unimportant. It is what I have done and where I have been that should be of importance. I have come here seeking knowledge. Some truths are so obvious that it's pointless to discuss them. I'm the hand up Mona Lisa's skirt. Never let them see you comin'. In the abundance of water the fool is thirsty. Sometimes you have to walk in darkness to see the light.

I warn you; I have yet just begun! If there is in your hearts a vestige of love for your country, of love for justice, listen attentively to me. I know that I will be silenced for many years; I know that the regime will try to suppress the truth by all possible means; I know that there will be a conspiracy to sink me into oblivion. But my voice will not be stifled; strength gathers in my breast even when I feel most alone, and the ardour of my own heart can sustain my voice, no matter how callous cowards may isolate and try to discourage me.

Men of respect blessed with wisdom of the ancients. If you don't stand for something, you will fall for anything.

Art is not meant to lull you to sleep, it is meant to beat you to death…. Artists should be terrorists, not masseurs. Art is not for decorating apartments. It is an instrument of war and should be used against the enemy. Art is never decoration, embellishment; instead it is work of enlightenment. Art, in other words, is a technique for acquiring liberty. Art reaches its greatest peak when devoid of self-consciousness.

Freedom discovers man the moment he loses concern over what impression he is making or about to make. Everything that is thought and expressed in words is one-sided, only half the truth; it lacks totality, completeness, unity. And in our willingness to give that which we seek, we keep the abundance of the universe circulating in our lives.

The past is history, the future is a mystery, and now is a gift. That's why they call it the present. Get off your high horse or die off like an extinction. Be bold and the force will come to you. Master the divine techniques of the art of peace and no enemy will dare challenge you.

Let me say at the risk of seeming ridiculous that the true revolutionary is guided by great feelings of love. However much I sympathize with worthy motives, I am an uncompromising opponent of violent methods even to serve the noblest of causes. There is no beauty in the finest cloth if it makes hunger and unhappiness.

We don't have education, we have inspiration. If I was educated I would be a damn fool. Men have never understood the words of the wise. So gold, instead of being seen as a symbol of evolution, became the basis for conflict. Everything that happens once will never happen again. But everything that happens twice will surely happen a third time.

If what one finds is made of pure matter, it will never spoil and one can always come back. If what you found was only a moment of light, like the explosion of a star, you would find nothing on your return. When someone sees the same person every day, they wind up becoming a part of that person's life. And then they want the person to change. If someone isn't what others want him or her to be, the others become angry. Everyone seems to have a clear idea of how other people should live their lives, but none about his or her own.

It is in exchanging the gifts of the earth that you shall find abundance and be satisfied. Yet unless the exchange be in love and kindly justice, it will but lead some to greed and others to hunger.

You will never be able to escape from your heart. So it's better to listen to what it has to say. That way, you'll never have to fear an unanticipated blow. My heart is afraid that it will have to suffer. Tell your heart that the fear of suffering is worse than the suffering itself.

And that no heart has ever suffered when it goes in search of its dreams, because every second of the search is a second's encounter with God and eternity.

Don't die of thirst just when the palm trees have appeared on the horizon. When you possess great treasures within you, and try to tell others of them, seldom are you believed.

The greatest risk is not taking one. Man created money so that other men can be bought. A sincere work is one that is endowed with enough strength to give reality to an illusion.

The greater masses of people will more easily fall victims to a big lie than to a small one. A majority can never replace the man, just as a hundred fools do not make one wise man. A heroic decision is not likely to come from a hundred cowards. They'll run out of bullets before they run out of hate.

Wisdom is not communicable. The wisdom which a wise man tries to communicate always sounds foolish. And in much of your talking thinking is half murdered. For thought is a bird of space, that in a cage of words may indeed unfold its wings, but cannot fly. Is your God forgiving.

MY END IS MY BEGINNING

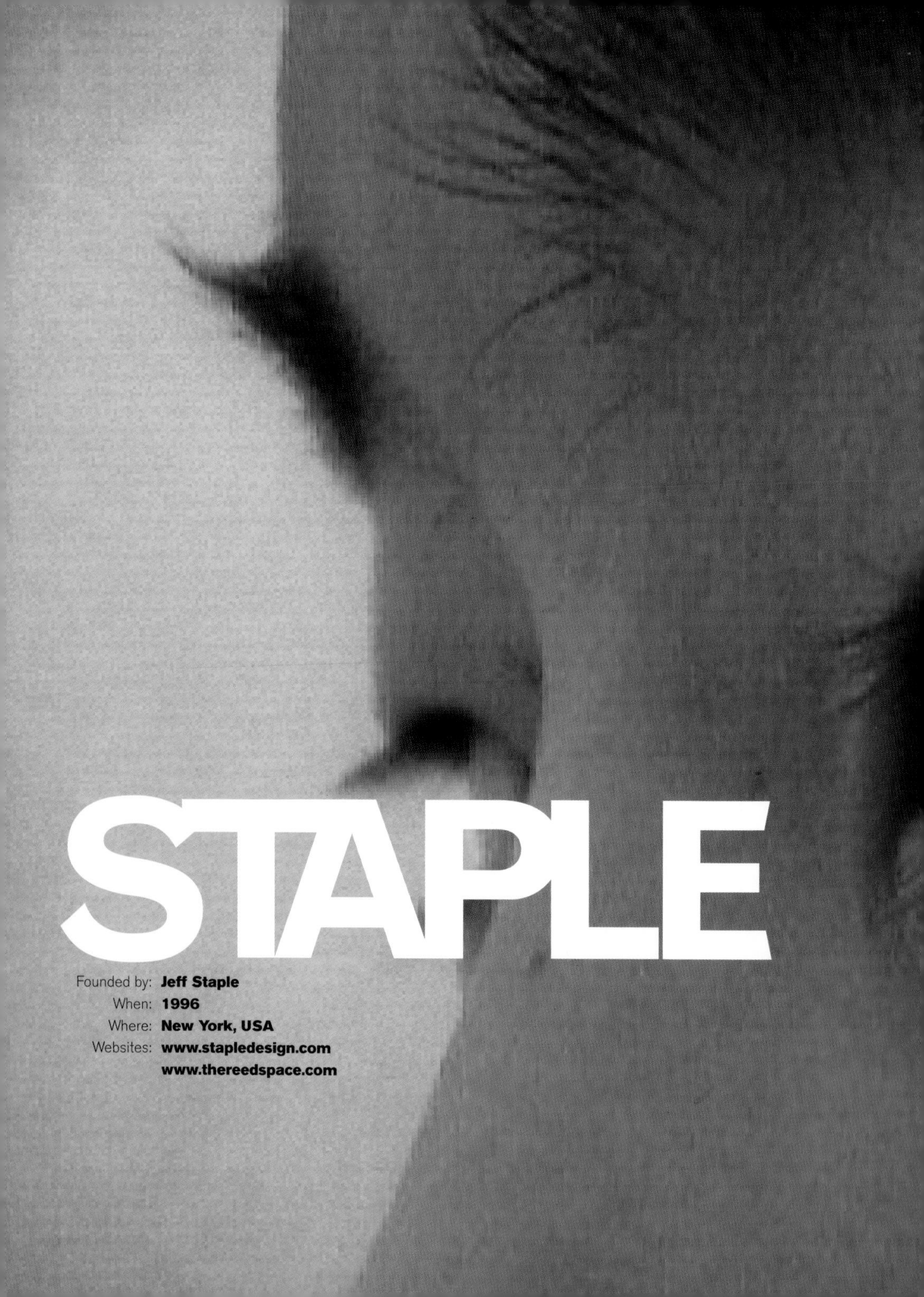

STAPLE

Founded by: **Jeff Staple**
When: **1996**
Where: **New York, USA**
Websites: **www.stapledesign.com**
www.thereedspace.com

Involved in just about everything, Jeff Ng, aka jeffstaple, has masterfully created an entire world of communication through design. The founder of Staple Design, Staple Clothing and the Reed Space is a graphic and clothing designer, as well as an artist, DJ, writer and entrepreneur. He and his team have worked with companies such as Nike, Burton Snowboards, Louis Vuitton/Moet Hennessy, Timberland, Uniqlo, Sony Playstation, Puma and many more. Jeff took his t-shirt business and developed it into a full clothing collection in 1996.

What does the term streetwear mean to you, from a personal and business point of view?

Damn, I was hoping to get some help from the dictionary. But oddly enough, it wasn't listed. I guess that says a lot. To me, streetwear is clothing that comes from the street. The operative word that needs to be defined here is STREET. The subcultures that call the streets their home are vast and numerous. Punk, skate, hip hop, rock. These are all forms of lifestyle that have their origins in the streets. So to me, a streetwear brand is anything that had its roots in the streets, or, in the spirit of the streets. Once you add that latter clause, it gets confusing and starts to open things up. After all, a lot of the things that Sketchers does are inspired by the street. So is it streetwear? Obviously, no. I think the other main criteria is that an INDEPENDENT individual or group started the brand. That element of struggle and hardship needs to be in the equation in order for it to be classified as streetwear. It is that struggle that brings about the authentic feel of a streetwear collection. Which is difficult to duplicate, even by the cleverest companies.

How did you get involved in this culture, and when?

I think that people who make conscious decisions to enter the streetwear market are not really streetwear, per se. Streetwear is something that happens by accident. If you look at the successful streetwear players, which of them had a business plan prior to the start of their line? For the most part, I would say they were probably following a calling they had, or a dream. They kept pursuing it until it became a legitimate company. So to clarify, I never made a decision to get involved. Or to enter streetwear. I started Staple as an answer to a shortage of clothes I wanted to wear. It was manufactured by my own two hands, way before it was cool to do things with your own two hands like it is today. I have spent the last ten years trying to be consistent and to find good manufacturers to make my line. Today, handmade shit and one-of-a-kind shit is what's hot. Ironic isn't it? This was late 1996, early 1997.

Where do streetwear's strengths and weaknesses lie?

I don't think streetwear has any weaknesses. I can't imagine what harm people think streetwear can pose. It's really not that serious.

▲ Nike Air Max x Staple Design

▼ Nike Shox

▲ Nike mowab considered
▼ Nike Pigeon Dunk SB

But it has many strengths: innovation, imagination, creativity, uprising and awareness.

Where is streetwear going?

Streetwear itself doesn't go anywhere. Its children just grow up. Take Ecko Unlimited as an example. Marc Ecko started as a grafitti artist wanting to make t-shirts. He started with six t-shirt designs. This qualifies him and his brand 'streetwear'. But his company grew. And changed its name to Ecko Unlimited and now generates well over $300 million a year. It makes video games now. He is an alumni of streetwear but has now moved on. Streetwear doesn't change. Only the players do.

After ten years of Staple, where will you take your label now?

Out of streetwear. Haha! No, I'm half-joking. My only wish is to maintain happiness while doing Staple and be able to put some food on the table. Good food, ideally.

What were some of the most memorable events that had an impact on you and on the culture?

The one that sticks out most in my mind is the Nike SB Pigeon Dunk release. Beyond the actual event itself, the aftermath of it was just amazing. After all, it definitely was not the first camp out for a shoe. And I'm not even sure if it was the first 'riot' that broke out. But the amount of exposure it got set it on another level. Basically, people that didn't even know sneaker culture existed were introduced to a whole new world. It was on the front page of the *New York Post*. It was on two of primetime's evening news channels. So you got some fifty-year-old woman living on the Upper East Side that is all of a sudden like, 'Oh my god. What is going on?!' That was really the defining moment I think for the sneaker culture. Its acknowledgment in the mainstream. For better or for worse.

The key to success in business is longevity. How do you see this, and how do you apply it to your design work and business?

A common business mantra is the five-year mark. If you've made it past the first five years of a business, then you're over the growing pains. Its not that you're immune to being shut down, but the beginning hardships that affect start-ups are for the most part over. After ten, its another echelon. And I think a tougher one. Here you are, pedalling this bike up a steep hill for a decade now. This is when a man questions himself and asks 'Why?' If business isn't going so good, then the 'Whys' keep getting louder and more intense. It really becomes a test of will. Fortunately we are doing well and its a pleasure to keep riding this hill. I'm in this for the long haul. So when it comes to business decisions, I make careful, calculated ones that are right for the long term. Sometimes I almost envy businessmen that have no deep-rooted connection to their company. They start them with the intention of selling them off in a couple of years and starting all over again. That ain't me. I wish I had a little of that, but for me, this is all my blood, sweat and tears. I've invested too much to make those kinds of decisions

What do you love about streetwear?

That's simple: the people. Like my man Bobbito says, 'Its not about the shoes. Its about the people.' Forty years when we look back at this time, the shoes ain't gonna be around anymore. The people will be. The stories. The relationships. Those are the things that really have value. It's not the shoe you slept out four nights for. It's that dude that was on line in front of you that you kicked it with and became friends. If you can't come away from this understanding that, you are missing out on the entire thing, kids.

▼ Nike Air Burst

▼ Nike Air Max 90

Creative Director: **Paul Mittleman**
When: **1980**
Where: **Los Angeles, USA**
Website: **www.stussy.com**

It is hard to overstate the influence Stüssy has had on streetwear and street culture. Many observers go so far as to suggest that Stüssy started it all and that it was the first brand to truly represent what the emerging subculture actually thought and believed. The fact is, for several decades, no other brand has so influenced, determined and set the standards of streetwear as Stüssy has. The origins of the label lie in 1980, when Shawn Stüssy, already a well-known surfer in southern California, started printing his own t-shirts, which he then sold alongside surfboards in his shop in Laguna Beach. Continually identifying new trends in music, art, surfing and skateboarding, Stüssy has remained at the top of the streetwear food chain for over twenty-five years. Paul Mittleman first joined the Stüssy tribe in the early 1980s, rejoined in 1995, and is now Creative Director for the entire brand. A native New Yorker, he has been involved in street culture since the early days. Despite the well-known dislike New Yorkers

have of leaving their city, Paul spent considerable time travelling the world and spreading the Stüssy message, helping it to become one of the most international brands in the streetwear industry today. As a result, Paul's designs and visions are seen and felt all over the globe by legions of ever-faithful followers in the Stüssy franchises and stores from Los Angeles, to London, to Tokyo. In a subculture and industry that is so difficult to define, Paul has achieved genuine influence, through his work, personality and participation right from the start.

How do you define streetwear?
I prefer the term street culture – it encompasses more areas of creativity.

At what defining point in your life did you realize that you were involved in something new and special?

I have still never defined what I do. I still think and act the same way I always have. My interest in music, art, skateboarding and fun have been with me since I was very young. I don't like round-table chats about abstract bullshit and branding. Unless a bottle of Jack is in the middle and we can all drink up and have a laugh. A bar or a dinner is my king of table. Being lucid and real is what street culture is about. The business of commoditizing the street is a different matter and should be framed and addressed in a separate forum. However, around 1986, I think a great wave of change in popular culture began to enable the business of the street and let it exist and flourish.

Where do streetwear's strengths and weaknesses lie?
I do not see much strength right now – I find all the collecting and

queuing up very problematic. I assumed the internet and websites could be a good thing, but they just dwell on what to buy. I would like to see more ideas and less marketing. Our biggest weakness and failure is not teaching the new generation. Most of the brands we covet are old. We need to collectively teach the young so that they can develop what we have carved out.

What memorable events had an impact on you, and then on streetwear?
The events are personal, but for me growing up in New York was a wonderful education and I would cite the Beastie Boys as changing our culture, and in a way helping to invent it, without even knowing what we (and they) were up too.

The key to success is longevity. How do you apply it to yourself and to your business?

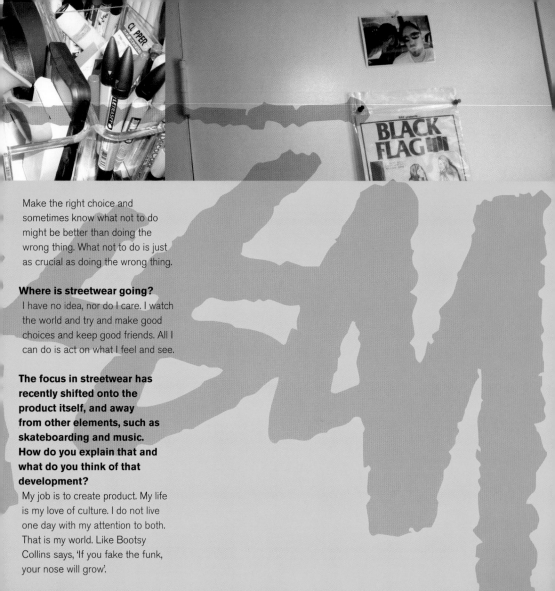

Make the right choice and sometimes know what not to do might be better than doing the wrong thing. What not to do is just as crucial as doing the wrong thing.

Where is streetwear going?
I have no idea, nor do I care. I watch the world and try and make good choices and keep good friends. All I can do is act on what I feel and see.

The focus in streetwear has recently shifted onto the product itself, and away from other elements, such as skateboarding and music. How do you explain that and what do you think of that development?
My job is to create product. My life is my love of culture. I do not live one day with my attention to both. That is my world. Like Bootsy Collins says, 'If you fake the funk, your nose will grow'.

SUICOMMI GROUND

Founded by: **T.O.Y & O.J.A.** When: **2004** Where: **Tokyo, Japan** Website: **No website**

Suicommi Underground is a distinctive new brand that has emerged from the Japanese streetwear scene. Taking individual interests and developing them into a unique clothing brand, the concepts behind this Suicommi Underground lie in the Japanese underworld and city motorcycle gangs.

When did you start your brand? What made you do what you do now, and who else is involved?
In 2004, art director T.O.Y and fashion designer O.J.A. started their first collaborative work together for the exhibition held at the The Pineal Eye store in Soho, London. The floor was full of elaborately decorated Tokkofuku (the uniform worn by the Bosozoku, also known as the motorcycle gangs in Japan) and the exhibition attracted much public attention. An editor from a fashion magazine, who happened to pass by the store, was impressed by our work and wrote an article about it/us. Then there was some guy who even stole one of the mannequins.

After that, we worked with some ladies' brands and held a fashion show in Tokyo. A view of high-end models walking down a catwalk and our models wearing Tokkofuku provoked such a reaction that we were convinced Japanese street culture could be developed one stage further.

How did you come up with the name Suicommi Underground?
We took the term from altered (customized) mufflers called 'Suikomi' which make a sound that rips through the darkness. Another meaning is an abbreviation of 'Suite committee'.

What is your brand concept, theme and philosophy?
Everything that inspires us is up for absorption. Suicommi Underground means the power to express things (which inspire us) in our own way.

Talk me through what is happening with your brand.
Our activities go beyond the mere mechanics of a fashion brand. We also create artworks and do graffiti. We don't restrict what we do, so that we can get to work with

▲▼▶ Suicommi Underground apparel

▲ Lamp
▼ Chair

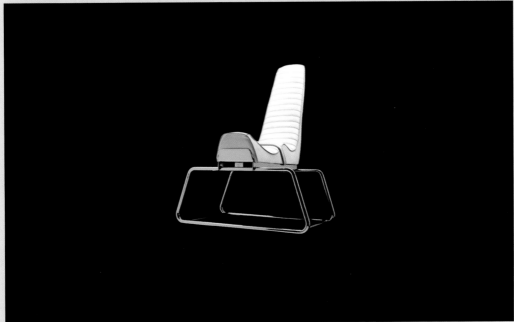

more talented artists. For example. there is someone who paints breathtakingly unique artworks on custom-made motorcycles, and another who creates hand-embroidery which is impossible to execute with a machine. At the moment, we only distribute to a few clothing stores in Tokyo and London. However, since we've been accepting custom-made orders from celebrities in the USA, London and Tokyo, our name has been recognized by the underground scene from each culture and our brand is developing.

Why do you get so much inspiration from Bosozoku? What kind of inspiration do you get from it specifically?

For us, Bosozoku is the original Japanese gang style, and we think it is *the* street fashion of the East. It inspires us because the Bosozoku put so much emphasis on appearance, but also on mental aesthetics. So we try to become a filter for them in order to present them beautifully and artistically.

Is there any reason for transforming Tokkofuku into high-end fashion and to then introduce it to other countries around the world?

We put emphasis on the beauty of detail. In order to make streetwear into high-end apparel, it is crucial to focus on materials, patterns, details and finishing touches. In order to elevate streetwear to a certain

level, we spare nothing to achieve good craftsmanship.

Tell me about the meaning behind the embroidered artwork.

Embroidery is the best medium for them (the Bosozoku) to present their philosophy. Every single design has its own meaning and expresses their existence. They are like an individual slogan, propaganda and poem in one.

What about the future?

We would like to work freely and exclusively crossing over the street, high-end, fashion, culture, and art scenes.

Interview by Yass Endo

SURRENDER

Founded by: **James Lavelle & Earn Chen**
When: **2004**
Where: **London, UK & Singapore**
Website: **www.surrenderous.com**

The Surrender label started at the end of 2004 and beginning of 2005 when James Lavelle, founder of Mo' Wax Records and the seminal super group UNKLE, met with Singaporean streetwear legend and icon Earn Chen. Earn had been running one of the world's premium streetwear stores, Ambush, for about four years prior to their meeting and is generally considered to be the cornerstone of the streetwear scene in Singapore. Surrender is a high-quality streetwear label with a subtler feel to it than some of the louder brands in the industry. Despite the fact that it has only been around for two years, it has collaborated on several special product projects with some of the industry's most coveted designers, including Neighborhood, 3D from Massive Attack, Kostas and Answer. The Surrender store in Singapore is a mix of ultra-modern concrete

▶ Bizarre beyond belief t-shirt

architecture, fine art gallery and the super-exclusive high-end fashion retailer. Yet it is not uninviting: as Earn indicates below, the store, like the brand, is welcoming, inclusive and open-minded.

What does streetwear mean to you personally, and as a business?

I don't know what streetwear means anymore. Personally, I would like to think of it as a lifestyle. From a business point of view, we hope not to be pigeon-holed as part of the streetwear scene, but work in all aspects of the culture.

How did you first get involved in streetwear, and when?

I started riding a BMX in 1981, and then break-dancing at the age of twelve, which introduced me to hip hop music. And during my teenage years, I was very into the punk and goth scene. Being born and raised in this part of the world, Singapore, there wasn't much of a scene, unlike the UK, Europe or USA, which have a rich background to the underground scene dating some fifty years back. So I was curious and interested in this underground scene and I tried to dig out as much information as I could. Until this day, I'm still learning and digging the different music, cultures and the underground scenes.

Where do you think streetwear's strengths and weaknesses lie?

The strength is the youth explosion that is the energy behind the movement. The weakness emerges when people start to exploit it from a commercial aspect. That's when shit becomes whack and dies off.

Where do you think streetwear is going?

In my humble opinion, I think it's going in circles.

What were some of the most memorable events that had an impact on you and the culture?

My most memorable experience was watching my favourite bands playing live when I was growing up, and being part of the movement.

The key to success in any business is longevity. How do you see this and how do you apply it to your design work as well as your business development and practice?

As far as design is concerned, we would like to unlearn from what everyone else is doing. And by using our influences and inspiration, interpret it in our own way.

And as for business developments and practice, we want to focus on what we do and not depend on the hype that is going around so much these days. I think we'll have to pay our dues to get there and we know it won't be an easy thing and that it takes time.

What do you love about this culture?

I love the energy.

▲ Lips t-shirt

◄ Femme fatale t-shirt
   ◄ Saturday Night Special t-shirt

▲ A Fistful of 77's t-shirt

Founded by: **Scott Sasso**
When: **1995**
Where: **New York, USA**
Website: **www.10deep.com**

Established in 1995, 10.Deep and Tenth NYC is a design firm and creative collective, of which the main output is the 10.Deep Clothing line. 10.Deep is one of the original New York streetwear brands, and uses bold graphics and quality design to create apparel that intelligently conjures thoughts of movements, individuals and the ideologies of days past and present. Scott Sasso, founder and creative director of 10. Deep, discusses streetwear below:

I've recently heard people describe streetwear as a direct outgrowth of skate culture, which for me is very interesting because although I skated in my early teens, my introduction to streetwear was through the late 1980s/early 1990s graffiti scene.

Back then it seemed like everyone had a tag. There were a million and one crews and the city was completely covered. At the time I was running all over the city, into every curve and crack and crevice where you could go to paint. During one of those excursions I came across a room in an abandoned factory in Williamsburg that was filled floor to ceiling with what I think amounted to a mission statement/spray-painted advertisement for the brand PNB. This was 1990. There was a list of names, a description of a way of life, paintings of standard-fare b-boy characters in their poses, and a signature that read: 'PNB Nation. Peace Out!' Mind you, it was still cool to say 'peace out' back then. Anyway, I didn't know what it was, or what it was about.

◄ Hip hop is dead sweatshirt
▼ The summer of no love t-shirt   ▼ Cross t-shirt

▲ Artists & Designers t-shirt

▲ Hip hop is dead t-shirt

▲ Beaverton t-shirt

▲ Boroughs t-shirt

▲ Logo t-shirt

▲ Stickers

▲ Evolve hoodie
▼ Tree Farm t-shirt

▲ Evolve hoodie
▼ Skull logo t-shirt

▲ Army jacket
▼ I love t-shirt

▲ Unsigned t-shirt

▲ 10 cent t-shirt

▲ Budweiser t-shirt

▲ New York t-shirt

▲ USA t-shirt

▲ Meet Murko t-shirt

▲ Pride beanie
▼ 1980 t-shirt

▲ Smiley t-shirt
▼ Chains t-shirt

▲ '45 t-shirt
▼ Cap

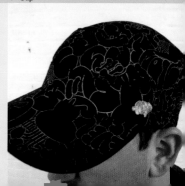

There was no indication that PNB was a clothing brand. I had no clue what it was about.

About a year later, sometime in the fall of 1991, a kid I went to school with started showing up wearing these different sweatshirts that had simple graffiti-styled, handwritten text on them with words like 'Knowledge' and 'Power.' This kid was the 'cool' dude in my grade and I wanted to find out where he had gotten the sweatshirts from. So I asked and he told me about Union. Actually he told me it was a special spot and he wasn't sure he wanted to give it up to me. I had to ask him about ten times over the next two or three weeks to find out about the store, but that's how it was back then. People wanted to keep their shopping spots secret so they could keep the exclusives to themselves. It's a funny precursor to what is happening now.

Anyway, Union, as you know, was the centre of what was the early New York streetwear scene. I went down there to check it out, and this forest green hat with a purple crown caught my eye. I picked it up off the shelf and saw that it read: 'PNB Nation. Peace Out!' I think I stood there for about five minutes looking at the hat and trying to understand what I was seeing. It didn't seem possible that kids could be taking

graffiti, putting it on clothes, and selling it. I mean, there had been that trend of customizing denim jackets or pants, or even skateboards with graff, but I hadn't seen anything that had been mass-produced. It just didn't make sense to me. In my mind, it just wasn't possible.

When I got home that day I dug up the photos I had of the mural in Brooklyn, compared it to the hat, and was surprised to see that the handwriting was the same. It blew me away. The fact that the people who had made the hat were graffiti writers, probably kids my own age, amazed me. I wasn't interested in making clothes at the time, but that was the experience that first brought me into the scene. It showed me the possible next step for my involvement in the graffiti scene.

Much of the base of the New York streetwear contingent have roots in the graff scene. Brands like Triple 5 and PNB that were the early streetwear brands (though they aren't popularly considered so today) included designers who came out of the graffiti scene. Brands like Subware and Project Dragon were founded by serious graffiti writers Stash and Futura. Jeff interned at PNB before he started Staple in 1997, and thus got some of his training from graffiti writers. Jest at Alife was a major

writer in the graffiti scene in 1992 and 1993. The only brand that I can think of that doesn't have a direct relationship to graffiti is Supreme, but if you walk into James's office, he's got art from Kaws and Rammellzee.

Anyway, all of this is to say that streetwear comes from no single source. Streetwear in NY is defined by the youth culture of downtown. It's been my perception that streetwear here comes from graffiti because that was what was big fifteen years ago. Three years ago when the scene was driven by artist-designed t-shirts, and having art shows in stores was popular, it seemed like art was the defining element of streetwear.

To kids getting involved today, it probably seems more like an outgrowth of skate culture because of what has happened with Supreme in recent years, and because you have guys like Pharrell who are wearing streetwear brands and also pushing skateboarding. I think what you see in looking at the history of streetwear is that its core identity is ever evolving, and I think that's how it remains relevant. That's why eleven years later I can still have a brand that is important, because streetwear is largely about the cultural climate of the moment, and our reactions towards, or against it.

▼ Untitled t-shirt

▼ Untitled t-shirt

▼ Searching 06 t-shirt

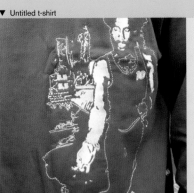

▲ Problem Solvers t-shirt

TWELVE BAR

Twelve Bar appeared from nowhere in 2004 and quickly became the talk of the town. In a matter of months, Twelve Bar achieved more than most brands can only dream of: press coverage in Japan, the United States and Europe and a brand awareness that was infiltrating the right circles, in the right way, all over the world. The main difference between this brand and many of the newer ones that have recently been established is that Twelve Bar has the quality, brains and initiative behind the positive vibes surrounding their brand. Nick and Damien's professional and personal past has enabled them to produce some of the most talked-about products of recent years. Nick discusses his background below:

Twelve Bar – a story to tell.

Back in the days when I was a teenager…. Before I had status and before I had a pager…. You could find the Abstract listening to hip hop…. My pops used to say it reminded him of be-bop…. I said well daddy don't you know that things go in cycles…. The way that Bobby Brown is just ampin' like Michael…. It's all expected…. Things are for the lookin'…. If you got the money…. Quest is for the bookin'…. Q-Tip from A Tribe Called Quest: Excursions from 'The Low End Theory'.

Six years after I was born, Grandmaster Flash & The Furious Five released 'The Message'. Seven years after I was born, Grandmaster Flash & The Furious Five released

'White Lines'. And nine years after I was born, Doug E. Fresh And The Get Fresh Crew featuring a then largely unknown emcee by the name of Ricky D. who later gained worldwide fame and notoriety as Slick Rick released 'The Show/La Di Da Di'.

I could try and pretend that this was when I first got into hip hop but, if I did, I would be lying through my teeth. Of course I knew and remember loving all these tracks but, let's be honest, so did everyone who listened to the radio or watched television at that time.

My love for the music really began in 1988 when, during an extended summer holiday in Los Angeles, I first heard Ice T's 'Power', Public Enemy's 'It Takes A Nation

Founded by: **Nick Jackson & Damien Webster**

▶ Peace to the Pioneers t-shirt

When: **2004**
Where: **London, UK**
Website: **www.twelvebar.com**

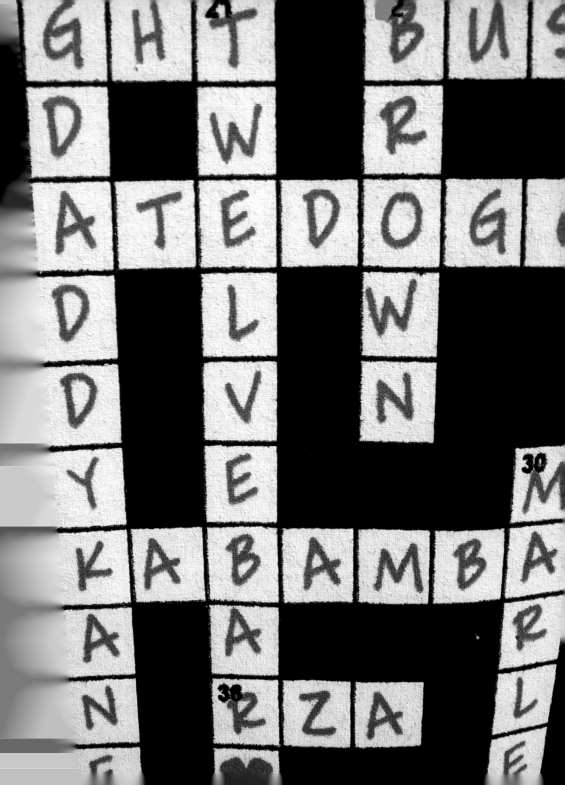

Of Millions To Hold Us Back', The Jungle Brothers' 'Straight Out The Jungle' and, last but not least, DJ Jazzy Jeff And The Fresh Prince's 'He's The DJ, I'm The Rapper', which I'm not embarrassed to admit I still listen to and enjoy now.

Aside from the fact that, quite simply, I was blown away by the music itself, which I guess is the most important thing, ever since the late 1980s my fascination and interest in the attitude and style of hip hop has grown and grown. In fact it was one of the main reasons why myself and my business partner Damien decided to set up Twelve Bar in late 2004.

Without hip hop, it's impossible to imagine street culture, as we now know it, existing and it has educated an entire generation about the rich musical tapestry that paved its way. Who on earth would know anything about Roy Ayers, The Ohio Players, Freddie Hubbard and George Duke, to name but a few, if they hadn't been sampled? Hip hop dipped its toe in the past to create the future and united old and new and this is exactly where its genius lies.

Where is this going and what does this have to do with streetwear, I hear you asking? Well, just be patient and I'll get there. One of the best things for me about buying new hip hop albums has always been getting home and reading the sleeve notes. Almost without exception, these are ridiculously extensive. Having said this, in the pre-internet world they were probably a fairly useful way of introducing new acts to those who study them diligently like myself. But, what has always been most interesting for me about the sleeve notes is that, especially in the late 1980s and early 1990s, the shout-outs would always be divided into two major categories – the 'Old School' and the 'New School'.

The Old School were the originators, the pioneers, everyone from Kool Herc, Afrika Bambaataa, Melle Mel and The Sugarhill Gang to Run DMC, Kool Moe Dee and even LL Cool J. The New School were the likes of De La Soul, The Black Sheep, Pete Rock And CL Smooth, Brand Nubian and The Flavor Unit to name but a few.

Obviously the New School were inspired, influenced and mentored by the Old School, but in print they were never belittled as being unoriginal or deemed less worthy or less talented than the creators who came before them. They were just the new kids on the block. The ones who had arrived to carry the torch as the time had come for it to be passed and they were deservedly getting the credit and respect they had worked so hard to earn.

As Q-Tip rightly acknowledges in the first verse of 'Excursions', the opening song on A Tribe Called Quest's sophomore album 'The Low End Theory', which is without a doubt one of the top ten hip hop albums of all time, everything goes in cycles and his words couldn't be more accurate.

Hip hop became the new be-bop and Michael Jackson moon-walked into the night to be replaced by Bobby Brown whose shoes have now been filled by Usher. Everything must change. The old inevitably are replaced by the new as time passes and it doesn't matter whether it's music, art, sport or even streetwear.

A constant phrase you hear bandied about these days in the world of streetwear is that everything has been done before and that nothing is new any more. This is something that sadly we spend quite a lot of time discussing in the Twelve Bar lab, and increasingly our view is that this is an irrelevant topic of conversation. Whether something is new or not doesn't really matter. It's all about how you execute your ideas and, whilst things change, one thing always remains constant – the fact that the good product always rises to the top. Quite what constitutes a 'good product' could fill an entire PhD thesis and is highly subjective. But take a look at the brands Stüssy and Ralph Lauren as two examples. Neither were the first to do what they did and neither of them invented anything either. Both brands have always released and continue to release distinctive high-quality products which stay true to the essence of what each brand is about, and this is why they continue to be so successful year after year.

Supreme is another great example. They weren't the first skate brand and they certainly won't be the last, but they have stuck to their vision from day one and made consistently great collections season after season, which is something that can only be achieved through hard work and focus.

Ultimately it's not about whether something has been done before or not. It's all about how you do it. Michael Jordan didn't do anything that Magic Johnson hadn't done before. Kaws isn't doing anything different from what Keith Haring did and Jay Z is only doing what Rakim did a decade before him. That's what we are constantly

striving to do with Twelve Bar. The name of the brand is a reference to the rhythm pattern black music comes from, which is one of our main inspirations, and our logo is our take on a heart and represents everything we are passionate about and everything we are influenced by.

Streetwear has been around for a long time and making clothes has been around since the beginning of time but we are putting our own original stamp on it all. Much like the 'New School' of hip hop embraced the style and attitude of the pioneers of the genre, their heroes, and dug deeper and deeper in the crates to find those rare breaks to sample, to innovate and push the boundaries of the music to another level, so too are Twelve Bar and a host of other new brands driving streetwear forward by taking our inspiration from the past.

We don't claim to be doing anything 'new' but who has ever done something new apart from inventors who own patents that aren't revoked! What we are doing is original and our own and that is what matters as, in every generation, good product shines through.

In hip hop, the Old School and the New School have always stood alongside each other. They represent different generations, different times and different attitudes and surely the time has now come for the world of streetwear to follow suit.

▶ Peace to the Pioneers t-shirt

ODMAN

OL

L

13 JAZZY JEFF 14 F

O

X

AFRIKA BAMBAATA

RZA

37 REDMAN

40 TUPAC SHAKUR G

43 CHUCK D

PEACE TO THE PIONEERS ©

UXA

Founded by: **Peter Huynh,**
Jefferson Pang & Peter Bici
When: **2001**
Where: **New York, USA**
Website: **www.uxalab.com**

UXA was founded by a group of three skateboarders from New York: Peter Huynh, Jefferson Pang and Peter Bici. Anyone familiar with the New York skate scene will know of these names, but for the uninitiated, they have been part of the skate scene there for longer than even they can remember. Having first been part of the infamous Zoo York and Supreme teams, they experienced skate culture at a time when it wasn't just a cool action sport, but a way of life. UXA emerged from this creative breeding ground as a forward-thinking and original label: their self-proclaimed 'motion' states that 'their graphic stimulates curiosity and enthusiasm and

▲ Jefferson Pang, Peter Huynh & Peter Bici

encourages an optimistic approach to the art of skateboarding'. UXA is also a creative agency designing for large labels like Burton Snowboards, amongst others. Their art installations are internationally renowned and so is their spirit, which keeps the real core of skateboarding alive in the twenty-first century. Peter Huynh answers some questions below:

Streetwear is a relatively new term for something that most people can't define. Yet there seems to be a collective understanding about what it is. How do you define streetwear?

It's more a term than anything else. I envision streetwear as evolutional or as behaviour adaptive to an environment. Like a tiger in the jungle; striped coat, fast, agile, with survival instincts. In the case of UXA, 'Lex' bear is the lion in that jungle.

At what stage in your life, did you realize that you were involved in something special and new? If there was one, at what definitive moment did you realize this?

(Jefferson) Pang and I had good feelings since the creation of Cream Skateboards with the opportunity that Rick Ibaseta had given us. The art direction was clearly different and we knew what was missing and what was needed

◀ UXA family & friends

▼ UXA x Nike sneakers

to form a modern skateboard art and a lifestyle label. Then the moment really hit me when I came up with the name UXA, I thought to myself 'wow'. That was it. Then ideas started popping up on typography, Lex, Skate-Man, Landed Eagle, etc.

In regards to this subculture, and especially in terms of the clothing aspect, where do you think its strengths and weaknesses lie?
I don't know, I tend to look at weakness more because the strength are clear in ideas. The weakness is how to keep it fresh. Most labels die out or go out with a five- to ten-year commercial plan.

What were the most memorable events that had an impact on you, and which then influenced streetwear?

I don't know, I'm so into creating stuff and making stuff; I made a wooden rubber band pistol at the age of six with my dad. I guess it all adds up, right? But when I got my first skateboard, my friends and I did coffins down and around this hill off Broadway and my first ollie onto a curb was it, kinda dumb but I was like wow, I can jump stuff.

The key to success is longevity. How do apply this to yourself and to your business?
I think leadership is the key. And with the right ideas, we will grow in longevity. I'm very lucky to have Peter Bici and Jefferson Pang on this project. Their contribution of ideas and hard work is invaluable.

Where do you think streetwear is going?
There's so many ways it can go. I like the 'fuck all attitude' of sex

drug and rock 'n' roll thing, e.g. Skull n Crossbones. The other is just creating from the soul, making things that individuals care about.

Focus has recently shifted onto the product itself, and moved away from other elements of streetwear, such as skateboarding or music. How do you explain that and what do you think of that development?
I'm into that. I'd like to collect Futura figurines, but it's always sold out. I also like it when things are made to speak to me. It's like it doesn't matter really, Reebok for example; famous for their 1980s aerobics shoes, now they make a knockoff 'uptown' shoe model in order to get some of the Nike clientele and it works. Or, Mob Deep rhyming about skateboarding, I like that. It's like the changing of guards.

▼ UXA x DVS/HUF

▲▶ UXA x Mutants t-shirt

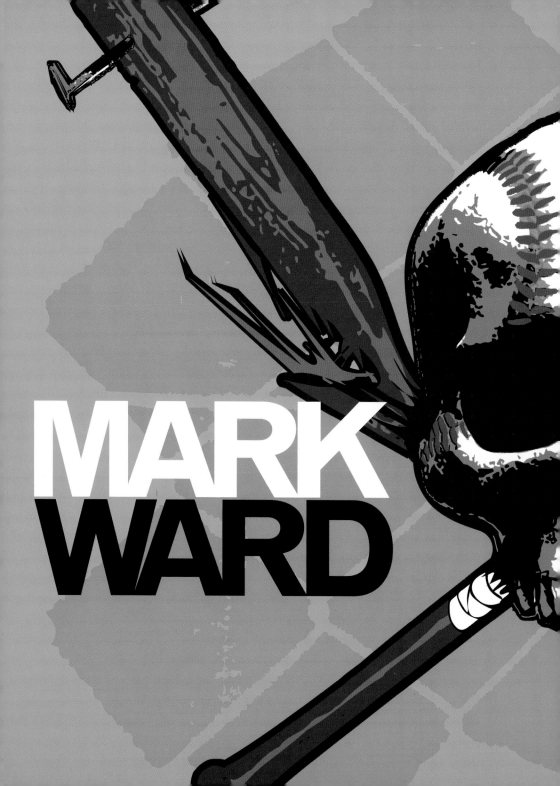

MARK
WARD

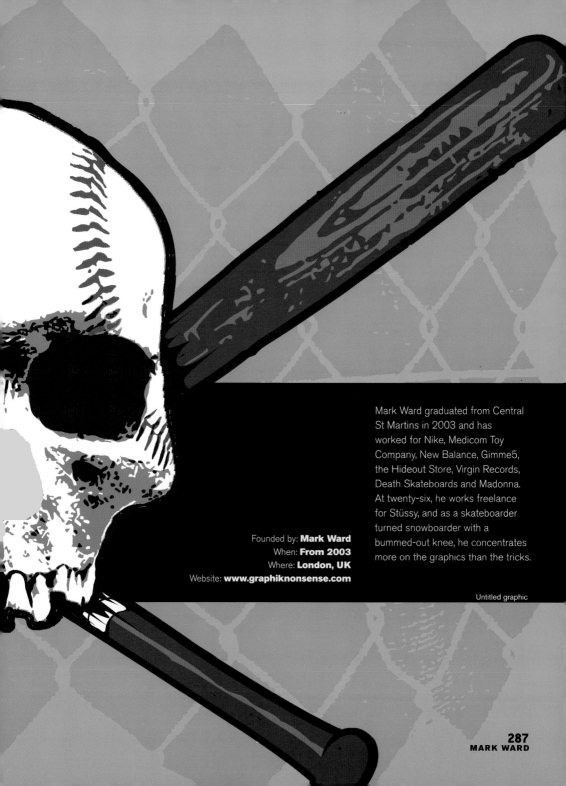

Mark Ward graduated from Central St Martins in 2003 and has worked for Nike, Medicom Toy Company, New Balance, Gimme5, the Hideout Store, Virgin Records, Death Skateboards and Madonna. At twenty-six, he works freelance for Stüssy, and as a skateboarder turned snowboarder with a bummed-out knee, he concentrates more on the graphics than the tricks.

Founded by: **Mark Ward**
When: **From 2003**
Where: **London, UK**
Website: **www.graphiknonsense.com**

Untitled graphic

Streetwear is a relatively new term that most people either don't or can't define. Yet there is a collective understanding about what it is, and what it is not. How do you define it?

For me, streetwear is an umbrella term for a lot of different elements. For example, skateboarding and BMX each have their own niche brands but both fall into streetwear, and there are also a few brands with a more general appeal. As long as a brand has true roots in an area of street culture it can be defined as streetwear.

When did you realize you were involved in something new?

When I got into skating as a kid, and a bit later into graffiti, I realized I was in a minority. Street culture gradually started to work its way into all areas of my life. When I worked a nine-to-five city job for a while I realized the rat race was definitely not for me, and that I wanted to be in a creative job that I felt connected with – where I'm at now has fulfilled that.

Where do streetwear's strengths and weaknesses lie?

Its strengths are that it attracts individuals who don't necessarily want to belong to mainstream groups, but on the flipside of this there seems to be a new label every week claiming to be streetwear; these are diluting the whole essence of true street culture and turning it mainstream.

What were the most memorable events that had an impact on you, especially in regards to the impact you then had on streetwear?

When I was a kid I always seemed to be trying to hunt down a certain pair of Vans or a particular t-shirt but could never get my hands on them! Ever since I started working in streetwear I've always tried to create desirable and relevant graphics as that's what I look for in streetwear.

The key to success in business is longevity. How do you apply this to yourself and to your business?

To achieve longevity you've got to be constantly coming up with fresh ideas, so that what you're creating is always relevant and wearable. You have to be really careful of becoming stale, though it can be tough trying to stay true to the roots and essence of the brand while appreciating the fact that culture and fashion are always evolving, and trying to balance the two.

Where is streetwear going?

I feel our niche streetwear scene will slowly but surely turn mainstream, as brands get more exposure on the internet and are discovered by a wider audience. Hopefully those people who get into it as a fad won't stick with it long enough to ruin it for us!

In recent years, the focus has shifted onto the product and away from other aspects of the street subculture. How do you explain that and what do you think of that development?

I think it's a sign of streetwear evolving. The use of premium materials, like selvedge denim, shows that consumers' tastes are becoming more refined. They don't necessarily need an obvious badge to identify themselves as part of the culture. I guess this makes room for younger labels to start up and fill the space they've left behind – there's a streetwear brand out there for most age groups now.

▲ Stüssy graphic
◄ Gimme5 graphic

▲ Untitled graphic

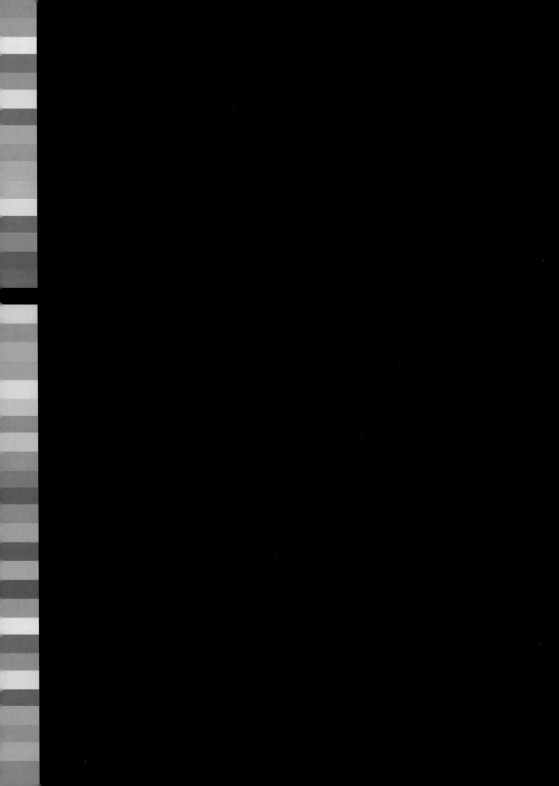

PART 2
MEDIA

Founded by: **Nat Thomson** When: **2003** Where: **Boston, USA** Website: **www.asilentflute.com** Blog: **http://blog.asilentflute.com**

A SILENT FLUTE

SLY AND

Nat Thomson, aka A Silent Flute, is one of the most straightforward and forthright contributors to the international world of street culture blogging. In his words, 'Street culture isn't that complicated a concept; it's basically just everything you've been into for as long as you can remember, all under one roof. It connects the dots between X-Clan and Butthole Surfers, sneakers and gallery art, fashion and hating fashion…. It's also a cool way to meet people that don't suck. In no effort to be comprehensive or objective, here's one man's A to Z of street culture.'

AAA VS. AMERICAN APPAREL

Deciding what kind of shirts to print on can be crucial. Everybody knows American Apparel, so when you print on their shirts, it's kind of blah. But they fit nice, if you're going for that kind of little-shirt AKA fashion-man look. AAA are cheaper and more on the traditional skate side of the spectrum, so you see them more. Then there's the real cats who design their own bodies.
See also: angel dust, The Artifacts, Agnostic Front, Animal Chin, Alva

BEASTIE BOYS

MCA wore Supreme to visit the Dalai Lama. Mike D invested in X-Large before it got big and they all had their own BAPE action figures way before Pharrell 'introduced Bape to the world.' And yo, before all that, they were part of the downtown party scene that laid the ground for most of this to happen in the first place. Top that.
See also: blogs, blunts, Back Flag, black jeans, bros, Bad Lieutenant

COMMERCE

There's always been a very real culture in all this street shit, but for people to pay rent and make a living there's gotta be commerce involved. More and more, this becomes the rub of the whole thing; selling to people who may or may not 'get it,' to make a living. Not to hot anybody's spot up, but these consumables are the byproducts of a creative scene, not the definition of the scene. So yes, you can be wearing head-to-toe Neighborhood and be still be a total douchebag.
See also: clichés, Carhartt, custom Air Force Ones (just kidding), Chucks

DUNKS

Tired topic, but yo, what was that all about? What started out as the mid-1990s chilly chill sneaker of choice turned into a full-on geek fest in two years flat. Now you can't even wear those motherfuckers unless you're going for that popular 'eBay look.' At least the backlash was funny.
See also: Dub, dime bags, Dip-Set, Doctor Octagon, dancehall

EXTINCT STREETWEAR

Pick up a 1990s issue of *Vice* or *Grand Royal* and you'll see ads for streetwear in its Stüssy-ish incarnation – cut-and-sew, accessories and outerwear, with t-shirts as an afterthought; Tokyo style, basically. A lot of these brands aren't around anymore because things cooled off as these growing brands started selling out. But then all of a sudden 'boom!' – a new wave of cats started doing graphic t-shirts with cut-and-sew as a luxury, like it's the 1980s all over again.
See also: El Topo, eastern conference, early 1990s, Evil Dee, Patrick Ewing

FUCK OFF

Seriously, fuck off. I know you know all the good URLs and 'rock' 'mad' New Eras, but how about you fuck off for a bit and give 'er a rest with all the shoes and shopping. What are you, Carrie Bradshaw?
See also: funny hats, favourite bars, fan-boys (you know 'em), front steps

GALLERY OPENINGS

Where, besides a house of fine arts welcoming you in to peruse the creations of a newly celebrated artiste, could be a more perfect place to get way wasted and chat up shorties? Openings are a staple locale for people looking to bro' up and throw up.
See also: Grand Royal, Glenn O'Brien's TV Party, grassroots

HIPSTERS

Hipsters are the retarded shadow of actually cool people from three years ago; they care too much about looking like they don't care at all, plus they probably have a lame job. If someone wanted to, they could totally do a 'you might be a hipster if…' routine, like your boy Jeff Foxworthy. For example, 'if you impress yourself every time you remember you like both The Pixies and Fat Joe … you might be a hipster.' Eventually 'weirdo' will be the new hipster, but for now weirdos are still cool because they smell and play mostly good records.
See also: Hanging out, hook ups, high tops, horror flicks, Heatmakerz, Keith Haring

INTERNING

What's better than free labour? If it weren't for the street dreams of kids out there, things would move much slower. Respect to all those willing to put stickers on every trashcan in Chinatown, organize 'really interesting' bills, and come up with good ideas, all for free.
See also: Inward heel flips, Illustrator, Ill Al Skratch

JORDANS

From The Bones Brigade in Is on through Puerto Rican chicks pushing baby strollers in pink VIs, Jordans are the king of street cred. There's this thing with Jordans where if someone steps on them, instinctively, people are like 'yo watch the Jordans, son!' It's a weird instinctual thing; pretty trippy. Actually, I think Jung did some work on it.
See also: Japanese Stylists, jumbo green tops, jump offs

KIDS

Mad movies get bigged up, from Serpico to Rocky and so on, but *Kids* is on some real shit while serving as a snapshot of the 1990s in skateboarding, music and partying.
See also: keeping it real, knowing good jazz records, kung fu movies

▼ DJ night

LOCALS ONLY

I mean really; do you want some know-nothing dick-weed coming in and teething your waves?
See also: Life Sucks Die, Love Park, Levis, Lenny Bruce

MISNOMER

Street culture? Nobody likes to be labelled, but at the intersection of art, fashion and commerce, there's something going on. It's like Wiley said; 'Wot do you call it?' Call it what you want.
See also: The Minutemen, Major Force, Magic Tradeshow

NETWEAR

Streetwear has taken an interesting turn in recent years: with the wealth of online resources and a low entry barrier, everyone wants to be down. Online retail has also blown up; gone are the days of searching boutiques for goods. Not really news on either account, but skip ahead to 'P' and you'll see where I'm going with this. Anyway, doing your own online t-shirt line is the new garage band.
See also: Not From Concentrate, Nostalgia, Nag Champa, Newports

OBSCURE REFERENCES

It's cool to reference stuff that everyone gets, but there's nothing more true to the real attitude of the scene than referencing an obscure record/movie/artist. Yep, even Zardoz. At this point, if you're still doing Biggie Smalls t-shirts then you're just in it for the money, and might as well be on Canal Street.
See also: Osibisa, the okie doke, open containers, Oui, outsider art

POSEUR

Poseurs are a street culture staple. There's a big difference between 'having it' and 'getting it'. There's also 'not giving a shit', which is the best look, so aim for that if at all possible.
See also: parties, Peter Savile, Public Enemy, Puerto Rico, Photoshop

QUAD

In Miami, a lot of people call Miami Bass 'Quad,' after the big four speaker setups used at parties. Quad is pretty much what's up though; where else does Kraftwerk meet long-butt bikini bottoms? Plus 2 Live Crew included one of rap's few Asians, and are one of few rap groups to get down with the Supreme Court.

RAVE

Rave is the secret shame of the street scene. In Europe they're fine with reminiscing about it, but in the States, everyone has rave skeletons in their closest (with safety vests on and everything). The novelty of referencing punk and hip hop in design is great, but let's cut the crap here; you were raving too, so let's break out those smiley faces if you want to keep it really real.
See also: Relax Magazine, reggaeton, Ricky Powell, Raymond Pettibon

STREET SNAPSHOTS

The street snap is a hallmark of the street fashion/culture scene. From *i-D* to *The Face*, to Tokyo's *Boon* and *Men's Non-No*, snapshots have become a global forum for street people, to see and be seen.
See also: Sonic Youth, Stüssy Tribe, sneakers, Sorayama, Supreme Clientel

TRENDS

Thanks to the internet, trends now last fifteen minutes. You've got to really want to stay ahead of things, and that usually means dressing like your bipolar uncle when he worked at a comic books store in the 1980s. In case you're into trends, just move to LA or London; that's where trends go to die, so you can just hang out there and

ride 'em out one by one. Nice hair gel, by the way.
See also: Track Bikes, Timezone, Taxi Driver, toys, Tokyu Hands

UNION

Before there was a street boutique on every corner of the globe, Union was the exclusive t-shirt spot. If you're not in Union, you just might be lame.
See also: Unique Clothing Warehouse, Unsane, the underdog

VINTAGE

Vintage gear is the secret weapon in the war on looking like an herb. In Tokyo, they get this; vintage gear fetches top dollar and gets magazine space. Not so much in the States though. Anyway, wearing head-to-toe 'fresh' gear just makes you look like a three-year-old at a family reunion, so chill with the crispy-ness.
See also: *Vice Magazine*, Vans, Vaughn Bode, Velvet Underground

WEED

Straight up, streetwear wouldn't exist without the herbal essence.
See also: Wu-Tang (doye), West Coast, Walking your dog in Soho

X

As in Brand X Brand. This well-worn path won't come to an end soon, but you gotta admit it's tired at times. Like when they make ice cream with Snickers in it, or Garfield fruit snacks. Are we supposed to really get into the crass cross promotion? At the same time though, it yields interesting results, especially when a big company who has no idea what's going on pairs up with someone who does.
See also: X-Large, X-Men, X-Games (maybe only kind of though)

YOUR FIFTEEN MINUTES

In 2006, it's never been easier to get your fifteen minutes. In fact it's pretty easy to get more than fifteen; I've actually heard of half hours, and sometimes upwards of fifty minutes of fame, depending on who you ask. With barriers to fame at an all-time low, it's a cinch; just print some t-shirts, get a digital camera, start a zine or blog, or just get your picture taken a lot, and there you go; you're the next Nico.
See also: YO! MTV Raps, Yoshida & CO, Yellow Magic Orchestra

ZINES

More backbone brigade right here, on some pre-internet steez. Editors, in general, have their heads up their ass, so for going on thirty years now the mad real among us have stepped up to the Xerox to pump out some informative and inspirational material. Think about it, what are you going to do, spend weeks pitching a story on your favourite band that nobody's ever heard of to editors who have numbers to worry about, or just pump that motherfucker out your way, yourself? All the best blogs still have that zine vibe that makes the whole thing work.
See also: Zulu Nation, Zig-Zags, zany (read: lame) designs

▲ DJ night

BEING HUNTED

Founded by: **Jörg Haas**
When: **2001**
Where: **Berlin, Germany**
Website: **www.beinghunted.com**

Beinghunted is an internet magazine that has been online since 2001. However, it is and always has been a lot more than just a website – it is in many respects a manifestation of the loves and interests of its founder, Jörg Haas, for a great variety of things – a physical object, an idea, or any form of creative expression. Jörg says that the philosophy behind *Beinghunted* did not just spring out of the blue in the months leading up to the October day when he first put the site online, but goes much further back, and is shaped by personal experiences such as the first time he saw a graffitied subway train in New York in 1985, or when he bought his first pair of sneakers.

Why did I start *Beinghunted*?
Because it is good to find what you are looking for but it is even better if you can share these finds with someone else.

Streetwear
'Street' is one of the most frequently used terms when it comes to describing certain aspects of youth culture. The fact that it is used endlessly and in all different contexts could be taken as proof for the absolute lack of meaning that the term carries today. Going back twenty years, 'street' could be defined as describing the opposite of 'water'. Streetwear was clothing to be

worn when one was not surfing … but skateboarding, for example. Other than the still common term 'surf wear', 'skate wear' – once popular, too – did not stick. 'Streetwear' did, yet the once more precise definition got lost during the years as printed t-shirts and skate shoes became more popular outside their original realm. Today, everything is streetwear. In some countries the term is assigned to the loud and pretentious hip hop clobber, in other countries streetwear could be the combination of distressed denim combined with a vintage rock 'n' roll band t-shirt. Streetwear is what people wear in the streets. And that could be anything or nothing.

My culture – their culture?

It is fair to say that *Beinghunted* played a major role in laying the foundation for a culture which has developed over the past two years.

The idea – maybe even philosophy – that drives myself, thus *Beinghunted*, evolved much earlier than the beginning of the website in 2001. I had been travelling to NYC or London to look for that one pair of sneakers or the one t-shirt long before the internet became available for private use. The web facilitated the search and the hook-ups between like-minded people across the globe. Finding someone in Tokyo now was just a matter of hours or days at the most. However, back in 2001, and still today, the internet for me is just a means to communicate. It never did, could, or will substitute any experience in the physical world. *Beinghunted* was and still is about products, projects, but most importantly people: meeting

people, travelling to and with them, searching and finding people, making new friends.

Beinghunted has helped to spark a cultural development that took its own root and has grown to some very extreme proportions in a very short period of time. While in 2001 there were only two or three other websites dedicated to the subjects of sneakers, clothing, art, design, or various other collectibles, the number of news websites, blogs, forums, etc. today is innumerable. Parallel with the increase of these publications it seems that the industry, the suppliers of the products talked and reported on, have followed this development of growth. While in 1999 there were two or three toy figures that one would have tried to organize from Japan or the US, there were hundreds just last year. While there were only two stores (one in Seattle, the other in New York) that organized art shows with young underground ('street') artists a few years ago, there are two or three openings in every major city all over the globe every month, now. While there were three interesting limited edition sneakers in 2002, there are at least five coming out every week in 2006. A lot to talk about, for sure, but it seems as if the spiral – more products, more news, more news-blogs, even more products, even more news, etc – has long reached its saturation point. Do people really care about the actual products any more? Or do they only care about the information and its news value?

Going through my archive and picking out any random piece of news I can tell its story, which in most cases involves a direct relationship to the people behind the project or product. I myself am responsible for almost ninety-eight per cent of the content on *Beinghunted*. It was out of personal interest that I tried to get in touch with that clothing brand from Munich or the footwear manufacturer in Tokyo. The features on *Beinghunted* are a result of weeks and months of communicating between various people, finding the right timing for a piece, putting together a suitable framework for an interview and arranging graphics and texts in the most concise format. Quality is still more valuable than quantity.

Tip of the iceberg
Beinghunted is an online-only magazine. However, this digital outlet, the interface, makes up for just a fraction of what it really is, of what *Beinghunted* has developed into. Through the site, a network of hundreds of individuals has grown over the years. This network serves as a playground and think-tank for new ideas. People from a great variety of cultural backgrounds communicate to work on ideas that will in most cases transcend into the real world.

From processing information, *Beinghunted*, similar to a branding or consulting agency, also helps ventures or individuals to create information, to initiate campaigns or to publicize them. Apart from just talking about products, *Beinghunted* has been operating an online store – The-Glade – since 2004 where a selection of items can be purchased. In early 2006 we opened our store Firmament in Berlin. A room to showcase products by the same brands, display art by the same people that *Beinghunted* has been

reporting on during the past years. For the first time, there is a physical space that could work as a walk-in compendium for the surrounding family members.

A development – the development
Youth culture seems to be developing more and more into a digital culture where people are spending more of their free time in front of a computer. Rather than showing off one's gems in the real world – breaking necks with that ultra hard-to-find pair of sneakers – people now post pictures of their deadstock pairs in their online diaries. Sad but true: only a fraction of the hundreds of limited edition shoes will ever touch pavement. The search for individuality, which sparked my own interest in all of what *Beinghunted* stands for, is what I lack the most when looking at this new generation. If I was searching for a pair of sneakers or a certain t-shirt fifteen years ago it was because I wanted something that nobody else had. Today it seems as if people want just that – what everybody else wants, has, or is talking about.

Beinghunted has grown slowly yet gradually. The interests have changed and so has the focus of the site. The main achievement of *Beinghunted* is to have brought together a group of like-minded individuals – all close friends – who are all working in their individual fields. We share similar backgrounds and we are all still firmly rooted in the 'real world'. The main goal and sometimes biggest struggle is to balance out the two concepts – digital vs analogue.

QUENMOVE

Founded by: **anonymous**
When: **2004**
Where: **London, UK**
Website: **www.cliquenmove.com**

Cliquenmove represents and guides both contemporary and original generations of streetwear enthusiasts alike. Taking inspiration from influential streetwear magazines such as *Big Brother*, *Thrasher*, *Dazed & Confused*, *Complex* and *Huge*, cliquenmove has adapted its creative genius online, creating cliquenmove. com. In doing so, it became the most relevant and international website catering to the streetwear subculture. What sets cliquenmove apart from other online resources, is its well-researched, well-written and well-presented content. Rather than offering a constant flow of opinionated information, it is instead laid out and reads like a magazine. Those responsible for the site speak here about the current status of streetwear around the world:

Online where?
Streetwear is in transition folks. We're witnessing a change. There's a new generation of buyers who don't care who did what, with whom or how. They're not interested in the history or the heritage of what is presented to them. They don't care who did it first, they don't want to know where the concept originally came from. All they want to know is where to obtain, download and order.

Let's face it. The world wide web has changed a lot of things in our lives, even though some of us wouldn't like to admit it. The new network generation are all over the internet. From London's Hoxton to Tokyo's Harajuka, we are being exposed to information quicker than ever. Its going to get faster, kids in Asia can see and already purchase products from their handsets.

The streets and the stores no longer dictate 'what is hot and what is not'. The information that some print magazines produce is far too slow. Blogs and forums are one hundred steps ahead, even opinion-formers and taste-makers have been forced to carve out their own window on the world wide web to try and show that they're still on top of trends.

If you didn't already know the effect the internet has, then think about this. The internet works just like the radio does, or did, for music. You hear it, you go try and obtain it. The desire for vinyl and the trip to the local record store was the method to get and use that product. However this method or type of thinking has diminished over the years, the recent record sale figures don't lie. I'm even witnessing record stores that have been around for years closing down. We now download or obtain music by other means. The physical presence of a record store is no longer required. Will this be the same for streetwear stores? How long can the instore experience last? Brands are now producing a faster turnover of products than Jay-Z did albums. What can the brand of yesteryears actually do?

Either make the instore experience unique or have instore exclusives. But can you make a business from that? All it takes is for an individual to purchase the exclusive and situate it on eBay, which has been happening for years. This kills the nature of the product being an instore exclusive. EBay continue to see their sales rise. But will there ever be a physical store for eBay?

On my daily scan of popular streetwear forums I always read this question 'where can I get this online?' Not 'where is the blah, blah store?' From what I can see, new brands are taking a new approach and are opening their doors online instead of at a physical store.

I propose the same question. What will the brands of yesteryear do? Stay with traditional methods or will they embrace the new generation's ideology and methods of purchasing. All I can say is people are no longer thinking local, they're now thinking global, or to coin a new phrase, GLOCAL.

COMPLEX

Former Editor-in-Chief: **Richard Martin**
Founded in: **2002**
Where: **New York, USA**
Website: **www.complex.com**

Based in New York, *Complex* is one of the most influential streetwear magazines. When it was first set up, there were concerns it would be nothing more than a series of advertisements for products by major investors. But thanks to dedicated hard work, expert insight and editorial integrity, *Complex* has become a firm favourite of the streetwear subculture. Former Editor-in-Chief Richard Martin discusses the development of streetwear, and of *Complex*.

The Shot Caller

The father of Japanese streetwear, **HIROSHI FUJIWARA** is the man without a plan.
By jeffstaple

Streetwear is a new term that is difficult to define. Yet there is a collective understanding about what it is, and what it is not. How do you define streetwear?

I define streetwear as a style that's developed organically for the urban environment. This can include tastemaker brands where the designer is someone who isn't formally trained, who is rebelling against the fashion industry. Taking it deeper, these brands often evolve, quickly, to the point that they can be worn with high-end designers like Prada or Marc Jacobs.

In another twist, streetwear is a style in which you can coordinate clothes with new, often vibrantly coloured sneakers or sneaker-shoes. An example of a polished streetwear outfit for a guy would include a pair of designer denim jeans, a skate company t-shirt and a blazer by either an up-and-coming brand like Trovata or an established name like Hugo Boss, topped off with a pair of limited-edition Nikes.

Where do streetwear's strengths and weaknesses lie?

Streetwear's strength is that it democratizes fashion. A designer doesn't need to be tied into the

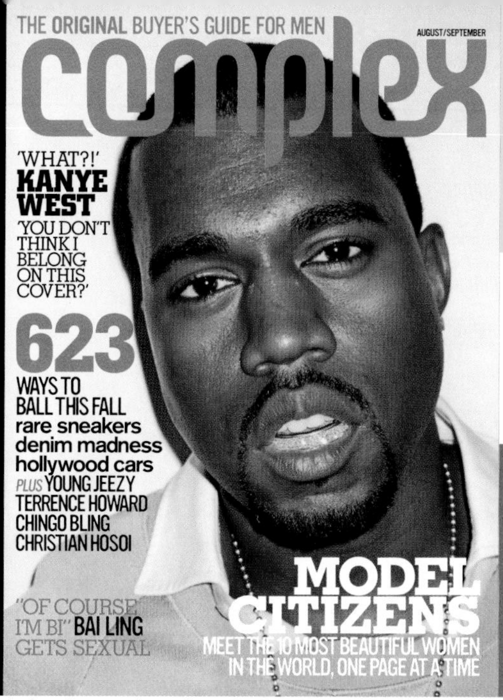
THE ORIGINAL BUYER'S GUIDE FOR MEN
AUGUST/SEPTEMBER
complex
'WHAT?!'
KANYE WEST
'YOU DON'T THINK I BELONG ON THIS COVER?'
623
WAYS TO BALL THIS FALL
rare sneakers
denim madness
hollywood cars
PLUS YOUNG JEEZY
TERRENCE HOWARD
CHINGO BLING
CHRISTIAN HOSOI
"OF COURSE I'M BI" BAI LING GETS SEXUAL
MODEL CITIZENS
MEET THE 10 MOST BEAUTIFUL WOMEN IN THE WORLD, ONE PAGE AT A TIME

▲ *Complex* cover, August/September 2005

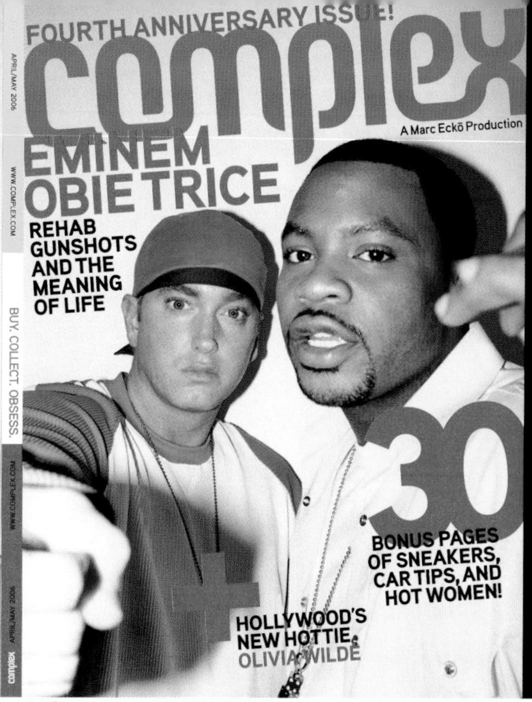
APRIL/MAY 2006
WWW.COMPLEX.COM
BUY. COLLECT. OBSESS.
FOURTH ANNIVERSARY ISSUE!
complex
A Marc Eckō Production
EMINEM
OBIE TRICE
REHAB
GUNSHOTS
AND THE
MEANING
OF LIFE
30
BONUS PAGES OF SNEAKERS, CAR TIPS, AND HOT WOMEN!
HOLLYWOOD'S NEW HOTTIE, OLIVIA WILDE

▲ *Complex* cover, April/May 2006

system – the manufacturers, textile mills, department stores – to have an impact. A lot of streetwear designers start out making t-shirts; if there's interest in their product, their sales grow and perhaps merit doing a full line. It's a more gradual process than throwing a bunch of money into something, marketing it and seeing how it works.

The main weakness is that the whole 'cool' thing is mercurial, and the tastemakers who supposedly define cool streetwear tend to develop the same sort of fashion elitism they're supposedly rebelling against, or at least reacting to.

Which events had an impact on you, with regards to the impact you then had on streetwear?

In New York, the sneaker craze has produced some memorable moments, from Espo's Air Force 2 release to the Pigeon Dunk release, both of which caused minor riots among the 100-plus guys waiting in line for stores to open. I ran a piece in *Complex* on the national sneaker phenomenon in 2003, and then wrote a piece for *The New York Times* on its impact in Manhattan in 2004. In the two years since the latter piece ran, sneaker subculture has become a juggernaut that has helped to propel my magazine, and dozens of websites, zines, TV shows and documentaries. Of course it has also aided the rise of streetwear as designers match colours to famed shoes, creating apparel that is inspired by sneaker colourways.

Where is streetwear going?

I've asked some amazing designers and style gurus, like Jeff Griffin, Eddie Cruz, Kim Jones and James Jebbia this question. Everyone has the same response, that people are becoming more independent when it comes to style, they're learning to mix and match. This is somewhat true, but you never know what cultural shifts will happen. In the early 1990s, hip hop and grunge fashion had such different, specific audiences. I think streetwear has closed the gap, so you have hip hop style and action sports brands as well as established designers all contributing to how a spectrum of people view style. When *Complex* started, I banked on the merging of skate and hip hop style at the

STYLE Q&A
AARON BONDAROFF

A-Ron the Downtown Don is a pioneer of DIY cool. His old stomping grounds became oversaturated with folks who missed the point, so he left to set his aNYthing brand and store apart.

▲ *Complex* spread, February/March 2006

least, and that's coming to fruition only now, like four or five years later. But that could all change instantly if some rap artist wearing a zebra-skin suit and white platform shoes becomes a pop culture phenomenon and sets off a crazy fad. Which is why I think the assertion that style will become increasingly independent is too hopeful.

Attention has recently shifted from skateboarding or music onto other streetwear products. How do you explain that development?

I touch on this in my previous answer, but certainly products and brands have become weightier in the past half-decade. I often tell people that a half-generation ago, to be considered cool (and to get chicks) a college-age guy would start a band. Now, he's more likely to start a t-shirt line. Items like the t-shirt, the sneaker, the vinyl figure, the hoodie, jeans – they're like a canvas, a CD and a billboard all in one. Streetwear mixes art, pop culture and commerce in a way that few could have predicted – and it's still evolving.

How does the internet compare to printed resources with regards to streetwear?

Because streetwear is such a trend-oriented endeavour, the immediacy of the internet has made blogs and websites a powerful tool to get the word out. Magazines have gotten kicked to the curb by some commentators, but don't forget that fashion stories often help gauge what's happening in style, and set trends themselves. Even in streetwear, the influence of well-known figures comes through best in magazines. So they're not only relevant, but essential, and I think that will grow. That said, as a person who controls a style-driven magazine, I'm aware of the internet's influence, and have the past year been developing a website that will become an indispensable source of information about streetwear. There are many sites out there, but most are run by a couple of guys and feature links to other people's stories. As streetwear continues to grow, readers will demand a better edited and more expertly curated source for their information.

HOOKED UP

Polo by Polo by Ralph Lauren, $65; shorts by Elwood, $65; hat by Blue Marlin, $29; scarf by Engineered Garments, $30

Polo by Ben Sherman, $89; shorts by Billabong, $46; watch by TechnoMarine, $1,850

SHIRT SHIFT

There's always white on white, but look into the new summer polos—crisp colored fabrics and all-over prints inspired by '80s graphic design.

Polo by Fred Perry, $110; shorts by Plugg Jeans Co., $38; hat by Kr3w, $27

Polo by P.A.M., $102; shorts by Marc Eckō Cut & Sew, $60; belt by Gant, $30; glasses by BCBG Max Azria, $171

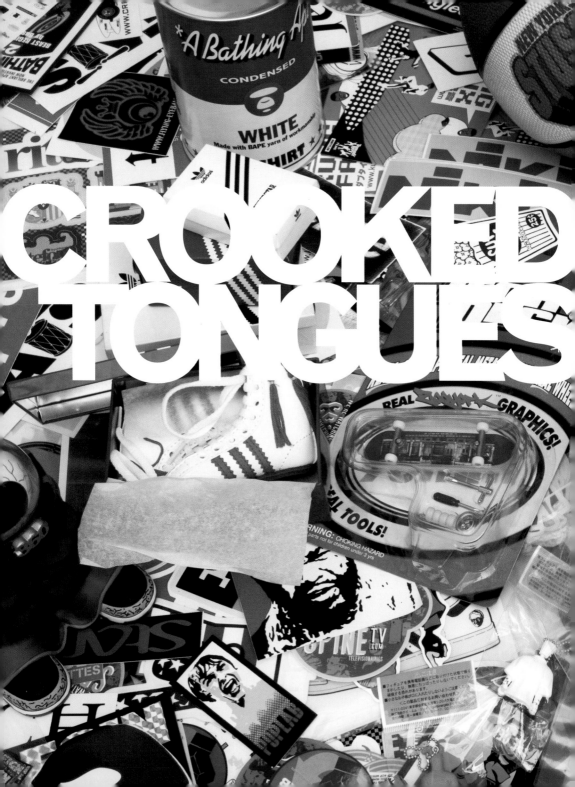

All collages by Crooked Tongues ▲ ▶▶▶

Founded by: **Russell Williamson**
When: **2000**
Where: **London, UK**
Website: **www.unorthodoxstyles.com**
www.crookedtongues.com

WHITE
Made with BAPE yarn of work...
★ T-SHIRT

adidas

SUPERSTAR 35th ANNIVERSARY

Unorthodox Styles is a creative agency based in London that has both nurtured, and been responsible for, some of the UK's most influential individuals in the domestic and international streetwear and sneaker scene. The well-known public face of Unorthodox Styles is the sneaker website, Crooked Tongues, which since its inception in 2000, has become one of the most relevant sources of information about sneakers around the world. Russell Williamson describes his perspectives on the global streetwear subculture, and shares his thoughts on the status quo:

Youth, or to use a more unappealing term, urban, culture was always bound to be jumped on by the corporate world. For many brands and companies, their target demographic sits loosely within this realm, so to see such an explosion of graffiti-styled logos, hip hop terminology and skate-related marketing is no surprise. Although there have been many subcultures that have been 'bastardized' by

the mainstream in the past, for the sake of keeping this text succinct (relating it to our own personal experiences here at Unorthodox Styles) we'll keep to a few selected examples. And so follows a brief tour through our minds, delving into the history of skateboard clothing, hip hop-inspired streetwear, the pedantic attitude of the casuals, and the ever-important world of the sneakerheads.

Skateboarding, or skating, was long dismissed as a 'fad' by those not involved. A subculture that would go continually in cycles – popular to the point of over-saturation one year and then dead the next. However, it never totally died out, but just went back underground like it had been in its most primitive days. Funnily enough, the same companies were quick to jump back on when popularity soared again in the late 1990s. Skaters have become accustomed to this though, and so have treated any media involvement with scepticism.

This time, there has been a more concerted effort to try and look less fly-by-night. Large brands, like Nike, have learned that the only way to connect with their market is to make sure they have the right people on board to help them. Consequently, Nike shoes are sold with regular skate brands, and the combination of technically advanced performance shoes has been balanced with vintage-inspired footwear.

The crossover from skateboard brands to more generalized lifestyle brands has evolved over the years. Supreme, once known for its skate store in New York, has become a streetwear icon on a global level. You're just as likely to see a group of MCs in Los Angeles rocking the box logo t-shirt as you are a bunch of skaters in Shibuya. But, to their credit, they never marketed themselves as anything other than a cool collective of 'heads'.

There was a time when you could immediately spot another skater by looking at his or her shoes or t-shirt. These days the mass consumption of skate culture has made it harder to spot genuine skaters. Until popular youth culture decides that skating is not cool, we'll have to stomach that for a bit longer.

Hip hop remains a potent outlet for product placement. Now where do we begin? Once upon a time there were some kids from Queens and a German sportswear manufacturer … blah, blah, blah…. You've heard the story a million times. But what became of them? Run DMC repping Gap? Hmm. DMC repping Le Coq rather than the Three Stripes? Surely something has gone horribly wrong? Does Funkmaster Flex really enjoy slipping on a pair of Lugz?

Regardless of bullet holes and crack-slanging pasts, not even a multi-national (outside the recording industry) could resist the lure of the hip hop dollar – cue Times Square billboards of Curtis Jackson for RBK and Busta Rhymes plugging Mountain Dew. Then there's the by-product of hip hop's entrepreneurial spirit. If white, middle-class brands like Polo, Timberland and North Face won't play ball, then they'll just create their own. Cross Colors, Fubu and Karl Kani were just the tip of the iceberg. Then, weighing in to get their share of the hip hop fashion dollar, there are the label owners and artists themselves. Taking the lead from Russell Simmon's Phat Farm brand, Puffy's Sean Combs, the Wu's Wu Wear and Dame and Jay's Rocawear set a standard:

regardless of variable quality and oft-lurid designs, these were nice little earners.

Of course, from lyrical gimmicks to slang, originality is hardly as sacrosanct as it once was within the industry and inevitably, the likes of Nelly, Master P, Outkast and Mobb Deep took the lead with their own 'designs' and declared their intention to sell their clothing brand in interviews

Through guerrilla tactics, if you're brand isn't 'down', for a set fee, it soon could be. Marc Ecko's Ecko brand shifted from t-shirts and mixtapes to the now-ubiquitous artist-led print ads until Ecko Unlimited became big enough to swallow Zoo York, release a 'tailored' line, peddle artist sub-brands like G-Unit Clothing and put out magazines and video games, in the style of a money-hungry conglomerate.

And just when Jay-Z's sudden middle-aged urge to wear suit jackets and button-downs seemed to indicate the time-old hip hop fad for rocking aspirational, upper-class accessories had reached its logical conclusion, things continued to develop. While certain streetwear companies evolved into a high-class model, other brands have entered the pages of the hip hop glossies with Kanye in Supreme, Lupe in Maharishi or Lil' Wayne in BAPE.

If you already feel that heavy demand has outreached limited supply, you ain't seen nothin' yet....

Many brands and labels now recognize their unintended association with Casuals and are unearthing old gems to tap into this nostalgic group of men teetering on middle age. Fila recently reintroduced some of their non-BJ, BJs, the fabled Munsingwear label returned as Penguin and adidas Originals reissued old favourites. At the time of writing there is a Fila BJ at £560 on eBay – a new replica would cost a tenth of that.

But although the Casual audience seem nostalgic, they can remember the most minuscule details about the attire of the day and have found (with either frightening recall or rose-tinted glasses) that none of the reproductions live up to the pieces they remember.

Brands that were positioning their product as sportswear, hiking gear and 'designer' gear were adopted and recontextualized outside the world in which they were meant to belong. These labels weren't targeting these lads through any of their marketing actions and this was one of the reasons that led to their popularity with this crowd. Somehow,

Casuals were above being marketed to – it was the quality and exclusivity of the gear that caught the eye of that crowd – not to mention the odd reference to Bowie or Ferry.

But ultimately, fashion loyalty doesn't exist with this group today and never has. Their turnover of labels may not be as frequent as it was, with brands such as CP and adidas

you ahead in the game and which item will complement your shoes flawlessly? Not every sneaker collector is into football, hip hop, graffiti or basketball and some of them have no cultural reference to feed off of. Where then do they find our inspiration? How do we carve our own niche in the market?

People have adapted sports brands as fashion items since the early 1970s, but that was basketball-based fashion. Sports brands had never thought about adapting their companies to fit with current fashions; they had always been about performance only, never really recognizing that a shoe could not only perform well on the playing field, but look appealing on the street also. It didn't take long for companies to cotton on to this trend.

Not until 1988, when Nike introduced its 'Just Do It' slogan line of apparel, did 'sports companies do streetwear'. Sports folks could just do … some running and other non-sports-folks could 'just do' eating a burger or viewing television. The vast array of people wearing the Nike slogan on T-shirts, hooded sweats or pants increased ten-fold into the

audience will turn their back and move on to a label which doesn't have the weight of casual heritage on its shoulders. The thing about 'sneakerheads' is that society deems it rude to walk down the street naked except for some shiny new shoes. So clothes are a necessity that sneaker collectors have to burden themselves with each and every day. How does one choose what clothes suit you best, which line will keep

acting as constants, but you can ensure that as soon as a brand chases this market the

non-sporting communities, and a global street wear fashion was born.

Recently adidas have changed details of their classic clothing and footwear ranges and made them more suitable for the modern, urban environment. Some of these changes upset a minority of the old-school purists, but you can't please everyone and besides they still have their classics to salivate over.

A small number of shops have started to reverse the roles of the fashion conscious. You no longer have to force yourself into an adidas track suit just to match up your Gazelles. Shops like Supreme and Undefeated, which started out life as shops selling other brands, are now powering ahead with 'home' brands flying off the shelves.

With the success of these companies, the sneaker collector has a niche in the market. Other companies such as Neighborhood, Footpatrol and Stüssy also succeeded by affiliating themselves with sneaker giants. However, the sneaker world is often very elitist and an agenda-driven market. Don't find yourself surprised if the new agenda clique is not to have an agenda at all and to have no affiliation either way. Confused? You should be.

The communication of streetwear as a topic is impossible to cover comprehensively in one article. There are too many individual moments that have made it what it is today, and the speed with which it evolves makes documentation difficult. As brands such as Nike link up with Apple, the merging of sportswear, streetwear and electrical entertainment is another possible avenue to be explored.

Whatever happens in the future, you can guarantee that as long as someone has the motive to silkscreen a t-shirt or slap up a sticker, there will be someone else waiting to write about it.

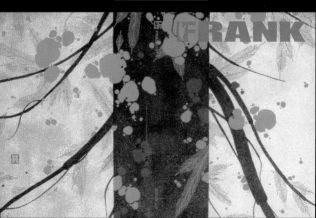

The Frank151 empire is most recognized for the intellectually and visually appealing streetwear publication *Frank151*. In addition, the Frank151 team also offers other services to the streetwear industry including brand management and opening concept shops such as the Chop Shop in New York (which combines an old-school barber with a boutique-style shop). Founder Mike Malbon told J. Nicely all about it in the following text:

Founded by: **Mike & Steve Malbon**
When: **1999**
Where: **New York, USA**
Website: **www.frank151.com**

Mediums: Sized Up
The streetwear game from
a media perspective

I have been involved in the streetwear industry for well over a decade now, and I have been wearing street-influenced fashion since Run DMC came out with 'My adidas'. Back in those days, I was growing up in rural Virginia, where it wasn't exactly easy to be a trendsetter. Skate videos and hip hop album covers were my main and only point of reference. From ordering t-shirts from the back of *Thrasher* magazines to finding a diamond in the rough at the local surf shop – we would dig and dig, searching all over to find clothes that fitted the style we were looking for. If we were lucky we would find that one design from a surf company with a street vibe. I was drawn to the style, but the product was hard to come by.

As I grew older I got heavily into snowboarding: it was a way to escape the countryside, and also influenced my sense of style. While at a Grateful Dead show in Madison Square Garden, I was discovered as a model. A scout came up to me at the show and gave me his card. At the time I thought it was a joke, but it panned out and opened a whole new world. Modelling brought me to New York City, and got me involved in photo shoots and runway shows, helping my sense of style to evolve.

At that time brands like Kingpin NYC, Subwear, Wu Wear, GAT, Phat Farm and Tribal were leading the movement, innovating, and showing that a streetwear clothing company could be a viable business.

A wee bit of snowboarding fame along with natural networking skills got me work offers and I landed a sales rep job for 90 Snowboards. This brought me to tradeshows like

Magic, 432F (the original innovator of streetwear tradeshows), and ASR.

The mix of snowboarding and fashion industries blended to help me define my own unique urban style. Going to fashion shows in New York and snowboard trade shows helped me collect a vast array of streetwear catalogues. No experience and a little bit of 'side hustle' money inspired me to open my own streetwear boutique in Virginia Beach, Virginia – the same area that I had spent so much time in as a teenager digging through racks of clothes. Now I would be able to offer blooming streetwear companies an opportunity to connect with my friends and eager kids in my neck of the woods. Coming back from tradeshows all my friends would always ask where I got 'those jeans'. Now I had a place to send them.

The Fly was the first true streetwear store in a mosh pit of surf and skate shops. The uniqueness of the store instantly created a buzz, and the local press followed. Teddy Riley, Pharrell, bands such as Korn, and Gwen Stefani would all stop by when they came to town. Insane Clown Posse even came through. That was where I also first met Omar Quiambo, who would go on to open the current king of Virginia streetwear boutiques, Commonwealth. Also, a young Dennis Calvero used to stop by – he would go on to start an influential line called Landscape, and more recently the up-and-coming brand Crooks & Castles. We were the first store in that market to carry streetwear as well as graffiti mags, videos, tips, and markers.

After several years running the store I decided that the retail game was a royal pain in the ass and moved to New York. Using my gift of the gab, I landed a Sales Manager position at what was then a cutting-edge streetwear company. I bluffed my way into a job with a burgeoning brand.

This company was the perfect example of what happens when a streetwear brand goes bad. After a couple of years it became too corporate and was gaining a reputation for not treating people right. As it started to fall off I decided that I needed to strike out on my own again. I decided to take advantage of the situation myself. Stealing and selling everything from anything I could get my hands on, from inventory to office supplies, to straight raiding the leather warehouse, I was able to move large quantities of product via eBay and raise enough capital to launch a new enterprise. Using the proceeds from my backdoor hustle I decided to invest in a new project.

My brother Steve had started publishing a small magazine while at art school in Atlanta. *Frank151* started out as a school assignment to create an original publication. His idea was to make a pocket-sized book of high quality. Steve had already started making moves down in Atlanta, and had even sold his car to print copies.

This project quickly received attention after I circulated the books amongst the New York nightlife and the downtown scene of key influencers in the fashion and streetwear industry. Using my connections I was able to bring many of these companies in as advertisers – on the strength of the book, and who we were as brothers.

Knowing both sides of the sales table allowed me to negotiate the best deals with our printers and advertisers. *Frank151* could be a platform to help these companies spread their message, and I began to gain a new perspective on the streetwear industry.

As I had grown up, so had the industry, and I felt that we were in a position to help a culture that we loved grow further, but in a sincere way. We offered a glimpse into the lifestyles of those who had inspired my brother and I, providing a platform for those within our network to proliferate their message in an unadulterated manner. This was when streetwear was becoming big business, and many companies were becoming spoiled by their own rapid success, or falling victim to expanding too quickly. Brands like Vans and

Burton are great examples of companies to emerge from the culture I grew up in, make millions, but maintain their integrity; I think that's why they have continued to support us. They aren't just a corporate entity trying to jump on the bandwagon. Sincerity. It's key, and it's the same quality that I have found and observed in the companies I have the most respect for. It's also a key ingredient in the formula for *Frank151*.

We started with a different concept. Rather than hitting the masses first, we focused on taste-makers and trendsetters, growing our publication from the ground up. With the ever growing demand for more copies of *Frank151* we needed to consistently get new advertisers to increase circulation. Using the same concept with our readers, we decided to focus on the best advertising partners in order to start a domino effect – for example once we got Nike, adidas would follow. Once we got Enyce, Mecca would be hitting us up to get on board. What we could offer these brands that other publications couldn't was access to the best most influential consumers who all had loyalty to our publication. When you pick up *Frank151* you know you are going

to get content that you won't see anywhere else. We regularly turned down advertisers that weren't up to par. To this day I still say it: 'we turn down more money in advertising than we will ever make.'

Frank151 has taught me that successful companies stick to their guns, and never get too big to forget about the little guy. Because the little guy and your core is all you will have at the end of day. While other publications revolve around covering what will make them money, or catering to their advertisers, we have managed to avoid that trap, which in turn has allowed us to continue to attract the most legitimate and respected street brands – up-and-coming and established.

In 2003 we introduced the Guest Curators, experts in a particular genre who would bring their own aesthetic and expertise to each issue. This kicked off with streetwear pioneer Futura. Since then we have worked with some of the best creative talent in the world: SSUR PLUS, Alife, Barnstormers, Dirty Doctor Daks and the Dungeon Family, Maharishi, Uncle Mike, Supernova & Situationormal, Nemo, NoMas and Haculla.

We have continued to increase our circulation throughout this time.

In order to achieve this we created the Frank Retail Network (FRN) and the Frank Distro League (FDL). The FRN consists of over 600 stores worldwide that distribute the Frank book to their customers and networks. These stores are chosen because they are the best lifestyle/culture boutiques in their markets. This is another way that we strive to maintain our ties to our streetwear roots. You won't find *Frank151* on a newsstand or in a department store. We know that our readers seek out the book, and so this brings customers to these stores that are independently owned. These retailers are at the forefront of an economy that is made up from the progressive-minded, forward-thinking global youth. Supporting the most legitimate purveyors of global youth culture helps to keep that economy moving and growing, and we believe that this generation of globally connected consumers is more aware of what is going to move our planet forward in a more positive direction. We try to keep this network strong and untainted.

This was the same formula that I saw in many of the streetwear brands that were the most successful, and I feel that as a publication, *Frank151* embodies that spirit and integrity.

▶ *Frank151* covers

MADE

Founded by: **Raif Adelberg** When: **1999** Where: **Vancouver, Canada** Website: **www.mademag.com**

Made is an independently produced art book. Published biannually in Vancouver, it brings together collaborators from the fields of design, fashion, music and art to exchange thoughts, sounds and images. Rather than an underground zine or a mass market publication, *Made* is a cross between a living room chat and a curated group exhibition. Yet it is also a traditional limited edition monograph with a homemade pop culture flavour.

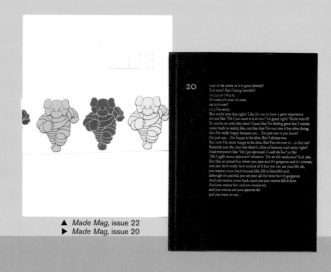

▲ *Made Mag*, issue 22
▶ *Made Mag*, issue 20

The Feast

There once existed a land of plenty. This land was bountiful and the inhabitants farmed and harvested their crops without fear of famine or plague. The gentlefolk would scatter the seeds in the traditional manner of their forefathers and the yield would be great.

The harvest was always the same; everyone was provided with ample provision. The same crops were sown every year as they were reliable and stayed true to the seasonal changes. The rains would come and the soil would be fed. The sun would come and the crops would grow strong. Every year it was the same.

The people would hold great feasts to celebrate the consistency and the abundance of the food. They would prepare the food in the same manner as their ancestor; it had always been so.

One year there were empty seats at the large banquet table.

'Where are our brothers?' asked the people.

'I have seen them,' one of the elders replied solemnly. 'They did not sow their seed with us, nor tend the land, nor reap the harvest as we have done this season. They are not present at this great feast; this annual celebration. They have struck out on their own. I saw them preparing their own and food and creating their own feast. Let us not concern ourselves with their petty experiments, but continue as we always have and enjoy our own great feast!'

The people cheered and the banquet commenced.

The small congregation perched at their own tiny table. They wore hearty smiles as they tasted the luscious food they had harvested. They had tired of the old ways; the traditional ways. They saw new land and news seeds and devised new methods of farming. They had been bold and, though no guarantee of success had been forthcoming, they nonetheless pursued their own path, feeling it to be right and good. They had endured mockery, but they had turned their backs and continued with their tasks. Now they sat together, the few of them, and enjoyed a bounty the likes of which had never graced the land. Every mouthful was as sweet as the purest honey. They ate and talked and laughed and agreed to try a similar approach for the next season.

Through the year, those select few imparted the story of the new crop to several other folk whom they deemed would be appreciative and respectful. Though first struck through with scepticism, these people were convinced to turn their hands to the novel seed. Again, they reaped a lush harvest. The feast was larger and had to provide for more people, but the food remained ripe and delicious. The recently-arrived people were struck through with awe and admiration for the new ways and the ingenuity of those few friends who had so bravely followed their own paths. Though they had not commenced the journey with these first travellers, the newcomers nonetheless felt privileged and honoured to be a part of the feast.

The following year, the congregation grew more numerous still. Those original few were unable to share their wisdom directly with so many newcomers, so others that had arrived to farm the new crop at an earlier stage imparted what they believed to be the true methods and thinking behind the seed.

These new people tried to learn but were more attracted to the stories of the bountiful feast that was rivalled by no other. They were not concerned with origins of the seed for they knew only that it yielded a crop unlike anything before; a crop that provided for great feasts that made those of their fore-fathers pale in comparison.

Word began to spread throughout the land about the crops and the farming methods this chosen number had first embraced. So it came to pass that the wariness and suspicion of the many began to break down. The intimate details of the crop and the feasts were shared, though with so many whispers, details and intentions were lost with each new seed sown into the soil. As its abundance increased, the origins of the crop slowly began to fade into obscurity.

Gradually the old way was all but lost into antiquity as the new method became the norm. The feasts were great and the food was good, but there was not retained in their preparation the care and the consideration first accorded the crop by the innovative few. These original pioneers despaired of the sharing of the crop as they witnessed it diluted and mistreated. The whole land followed the new way.

This continued for years and years. Generation after generation handed down the methods of sowing and farming the new crop. The people of the land became adept at the production and the harvest of the crop on a grand scale. Each year the feast brought great joy to everyone in the land. Then, one day, it became apparent that there were a small number of empty seats at the large banquet table.

'Where are our brothers?' asked the people.

MADE MAGAZINE

the

FEAST

A CAUTIONARY TALE

VAPORS

Founded by: **Jason Maggio**   When: **2000**   Where: **San Francisco, USA**   Website: **www.vaporsmagazine.com**

Vapors, or as it is properly known, *Vapors, All City Magazine*, is one of the few relevant publications in the streetwear subculture, due to the ever fighting, fiercely independent yet highly professional personality of founder and former Editor-in-Chief Jason Maggio. Through his publication, which quickly established itself as a mouthpiece for a generation of skaters, graffiti writers and music lovers, at first predominantly based on the West Coast and subsequently around the world, Jason has had his finger on streetwear's pulse, mostly because he is as much a part of it as this sub culture is a part of him. His opinions and ideas are highly relevant, and he provides in the following essay a glimpse of what shaped his life and his career:

The term 'streetwear' is a bit ambiguous. Its definition, history, current and future state are argued tirelessly amongst self-appointed street culture aficionados to the point of exhaustion and delusion. Being involved in an industry that thrives off this term, it's safe to say I have some educated opinions on the subject. But when I ask myself, 'What is streetwear?' my answer is more dictated by my experiences, my style and my own desire to dress in a fashion that represents where and who I am, than a label used to commodify a culture and sell advertisements in magazines. What is streetwear? It's you – utilizing fabric and fashion sense to represent your perspective on the street and how the street made you the person you are today.

A glimpse into one of my own experiences and fashion phases might better paint a picture of what streetwear is to me. Back in 1992 I was twenty years old, up a lot in my city (graff-wise) and beginning to feel a magnetic pull towards the freight yards. The romanticism of the reconnaissance necessary, cat and mouse games with Southern Pacific police and the potential to go 'All Nation' drew me to the yards many a night. One particular night I rolled out to the infamous Roseville yard (one of the largest and busiest freight yards west of the Mississippi). The cat I was rolling with had maps of Roseville yard and all kinds of Roseville folklore in his room. The kid was obsessed with this yard, had been there hundreds of times and memorized every single entry and exit including a canyon, filled waist-deep in toxic sludge (only to be used as a last-resort escape). I, on the flip side, had never ventured into Roseville and was a little hesitant because of its notoriety. Barring good judgment I zipped up my US Army BDU Gore-Tex jacket that matched my BDU pants (one leg rolled up, à la Wu Tang circa 1992), laced up the black 574 New Balances tight in case we had to cut, filled up the black Eastpak with fifteen new cans, pulled up the black Neoprene ski mask over my nose, wished I had some night vision goggles and dropped in (for lack of a better term). About the tenth car in and working on a little four-colour floater my partner signals to hide and I fosberry flop (high jump steez) into a boxcar likkety-split. Five long minutes go by and dude comes over laughing his ass off at how shook up I was. At the end of his hysteric, evil banter he informed me that he was just playin'. I failed to see the humour and had suddenly lost my enthusiasm to carry out the bombing agenda for the evening.

As he reluctantly and I enthusiastically made our way back to the car we heard the faint sound of Quadrunners (the cop's vehicle of choice in the yard) making their way toward us a few sets of track over. With no plan intact, we scrambled in haste and unfortunately in different directions. As the cops got closer I ducked behind some steel wheels moth-balled on the side of the tracks and literally dug into the soot and oil-coated gravel for cover. It was a mid-December foggy night and the bone-cold chill was intensified when lying on the ground. I could see the cops piecing our puzzle together and contemplating our escape route.

The tower dispatched more cops and all of a sudden the yard was abuzz with that frightful surround-sound hum of Quadrunners. To my amazement my partner finds me and he digs in under the axles of these discarded wheels with me. Instantly, searchlights illuminated our perimeter and it was a matter of time before we were hemmed up. As the search continued I learned that this camouflage (my jacket, pants, mask) and our instant foxhole was testing the resolve of the SP cops. It became a game of them smoking us out. They maintained the perimeter knowing that we were not out of the yard and held tight waiting for our surrender. After two strenuous hours of laying on the ground my partner wants to throw up the white flag, downplaying the potential punishment and complaining that all feeling in his toes was lost. I was bound and determined to wait it out and hope for a lull in the shift change to make our escape. I begged him not to give up. This was a test of our wills and the consequences of being caught were far worse than a little frostbite. My Gore-Tex US Army jacket was keeping me snug and hidden from the fuzz and in my emerging frozen delirium I was grateful to Shaolin, the Grave Diggas, SEEN, Bucktown, LOTNS and Vietnam vets for inspiring me to drop $150 on an Army jacket and not some flashy reflective, silver Hilfiger puffy coat that all the rap stars seemed to be rocking that winter. Life was not about Bentleys, speedboats and Lear jets. It was about getting up and surviving. Surviving the yard, no matter what it throws at you, builds character, credibility and ultimately you will carry those trials and

tribulations as street culture medals for the rest of your life. Aptly, I was dressed head-to-toe in medal-earning gear.

To make a long escape story short…. We did make it out of the yard just before dawn and when we tasted freedom (the heater air in the car) we instantly became men in a kid's world. We could conquer anything and were eager to tell our friends and foes just that. The next night at the club guess what I was rocking? That same Army Gore-Tex jacket, pants (one leg up of course), my 574s and a Neoprene ski mask to let heads know I was a bandit, a vandal, a mutherfucking yardie.

Nowadays I just laugh…. Wear that silk-scarf shit to the yard and you might get dropped.

PART
3
RESOURCES

AFTERWORD

Throughout the process of creating this book, my mind has been on constant overdrive, always unconsciously (and sometimes even consciously) thinking about the subject of streetwear and street culture. There have been numerous times of self-doubt about both of those subjects – it has been a real and very emotional rollercoaster ride.

The majority of questions that preoccupied not only my mind, but also those of many of the participants in, and contributors to, this book, focused on the major issues: what is the purpose of talking about something that is, by its very nature, almost indefinable? And how do you pin down something so alive as street culture and which is as constantly evolving as global streetwear?

Those questions have always bugged me throughout my involvement in the subculture, especially as a writer. They still bug me now.

This book does not set out to define, or even give the final word on what the word streetwear means. Nor, taking the issue to another level, does it aim to draw up a single definition so that depending on each of our individual positions, certain clothes, brands and people are thought of as being 'streetwear' or indeed, 'not streetwear'.

Definitions, in my opinion, are limiting to the imagination, and in many respects quite dangerous, since they can inhibit our ability to look beyond any self-imposed view of the world. Yet the need to define, catalogue, order and 'put in a box', seems to be an integral part of human nature. Definitions provide us with a means to place or position our identity in relation to others, and in terms of a subculture – such as street culture – this is a driving factor, since the majority of the participants in this subculture are young. And nothing is more important to a young person than to identify with a certain group, or a set of ideals you share with that group.

As one gets older, these clear definitions tend to blur, and the self-imposed constructs built within those definitions start to fracture. Ironically, street culture, which is often rendered in what people think of as streetwear, was always the antithesis of a predefined world – it was the spirit of punk; it was an anti-authoritarian state of mind; it was the sense of freedom you can get from skateboarding. The expression of those ideals in the music and art that has emerged from street culture are all about breaking down definitions and freeing yourself from preset blueprints that others follow.

So streetwear cannot and should not be defined, and this book, while providing a snapshot of the most creative, exciting and dynamic work being produced right now by those immersed in the subculture, doesn't set out to make any definitions or draw any lines in the sand. What I have tried to do is share the knowledge amongst those within the subculture, and for those looking from the outside, offer a sense of understanding in terms of 'this is who we are, and this is what we do'. This book is a slice through a complex subculture rooted in a common feeling of freedom, fun and fascination with the world at large.

Put simply, through interviews and short stories by and with my friends (some of whom share the ideas I have and choose to express them in the same way as I do), I have tried to capture the essence of what makes streetwear tick — to tell you something about its soul.

Streetwear is not about what you wear or how you wear it, but is a common set of ideals and experiences expressed visually and physically in the art and clothes that those who are part of the subculture produce. With streetwear, it's the feeling that counts.

So, to return to what has bugged me for years: how do you define the indefinable? I know I've learnt this much from putting the book together — this book is not a 'who's who in streetwear', that would be impossible to complete as there are so many people out there, creating things and enjoying the freedom of the subculture that you could never capture them in a jar. The scene is evolving and changing so fast, that neither could you set it in stone. Instead, this book is intended to be a collection of ideas and thoughts on the subject, suitable for a round-table discussion with your friends over a barbecue and beers after a

good day's skating. In essence, it is a talking point about what this thing that is a home to us all involves. For those of you who have come to the subculture fresh from the outside, I hope that without giving you a definition, all of us here have been able to give you a clearer understanding of what and why we do the things we do.

I leave you with a quote by Robert Delauney which I have always enjoyed, and distils much of what troubles me of the need to 'define':

'I am very much afraid of definitions, and yet one is almost forced to make them. One must take care, too, not to be inhibited by them'. Robert Delauney

Steven Vogel
Berlin, October 2006

GLOBAL STORE DIRECTORY

The stores listed below in no way represent every streetwear boutique or shop that exists throughout the world. They should, however, provide a good starting and reference point for where to buy streetwear in relevant major cities.

AUSTRALIA

Stüssy
Chadstone Shopping Centre
1341 Dandenong Road
Chadstone
Victoria 3148
Australia
www.stussy.com

Supply
Basement Store
20 Burton Street
Darlinghurst, Sydney
NSW 2010
Australia

AUSTRIA

Stil-Laden
Lindengasse 51/21070
Vienna
Austria
www.stil-laden.at

BELGIUM

Alice
182 Rue Antoine Dansaert,
Brussels 1000
Belgium
www.alicebxl.com

Hype Shop
Rijke Klarenstraat 4
Brussels 1000
Belgium
www.hypeshop.com

CANADA

Alife Vancouver
350 Water Street
Vancouver BC, V6B 1E2
Canada
www.alifenyc.com

Foosh
10544C 82nd Avenue NW
Edmonton AB, T6E 2A4
Canada
www.foosh.ca

Goodfoot
3830 St. Laurent Boulevard
Montreal QC, H2W 1X6
Canada

431 Richmond Street West
Toronto ON, M5V 1X9
Canada
www.getonthegoodfoot.ca

Headquarter
1232 Burrard Street
Vancouver BC, V6Z 1Z1
Canada
www.headquarterstore.com

Livestock
239 Abbott Street
Vancouver BC, V6B 2K7
Canada
www.deadstock.ca

Nomad
431 Richmond Street
West Toronto ON, M5V 1X9
Canada
www.nomadshop.net

Subdivision
Unit 2, 306 Water Street
Vancouver BC, V6B 1B6
Canada
www.subdivisioninc.com

Uncle Otis
26 Bellair Street
Toronto ON, M5R 2C7
Canada
www.uncleotis.com

CHINA

852
United Success Commercial Centre
506/508 Jaffe Road
Causeway Bay, Hong Kong
China

Dusty
86 Fa Yuen Street
Mongkok, Hong Kong
China
www.dusty.com.hk

Juice
53 Paterson Street
Causeway Bay, Hong Kong
China

Medium Rare
545 Lockhart Road [1st floor]
Causeway Bay, Hong Kong
China

Overhead 1
20 Percival Road
Causeway Bay, Hong Kong
China

Stüssy
Shop C & D 121–123
Chatham Road, Tsim Sha Tsui
Kowloon, Hong Kong
China
www.stussy.com

DENMARK

Norse
Teglgaardstraede 6A
1452 Copenhagen K
Denmark
www.norsestore.com

WoodWood
Krystalgade 4 & 7
1172 Copenhagen
Denmark
www.woodwood.dk

FRANCE

Colette
213 rue Saint-Honoré
Paris 75001
France
www.colette.fr

The Lazy Dog
2 Passage Thiere
Paris 75011
France
www.thelazydog.fr

Opium
9 rue du Cygne
Paris 75001
France
www.opiumstore.com

Starcow
68 rue Saint-Honoré
Paris 75001
France
http://starcow.over-blog.com

GERMANY

Firmament
Schröderstrasse 8
10115 Berlin
Germany
www.am-firmament.com

Kickback
Gärtnerstrasse, 3110245 Berlin
Germany
www.kickback-berlin.com

Nort
Münzstrasse, 1910178 Berlin
Germany
www.nortberlin.com

Solebox
Nürnbergerstrasse
1610789 Berlin
Germany
www.solebox.de

T.A.T.E
Gänsemarkt
2420345 Hamburg
Germany

Vibes
Mittelstrasse16
40213 Düsseldorf
Germany

Ehrenstrasse
7350627 Cologne
Germany
www.vibes-store.de

Thomas-i-Punkt
Mönckebergstrasse 2120095
Hamburg
Germany

ITALY

Slam Jam
Via Canonica 12
Ferrera
Italy
www.slamjamstore.it

Stüssy
C.So Di Porta Ticinese
10320100 Milano
Italy
www.stussy.com

JAPAN

Base Station
6–5–6 Jingumae
Shibuya-ku, Tokyo 150–0001
Japan
www.basestation.jp

Blackflag
5–4–24 1F Minami-Aoyama
Minato-Ku, Tokyo
Japan

Bounty Hunter
3–15–8 Jingumae
Shibuya-ku, Tokyo 150–0001
Japan
www.bounty-hunter.com

Foot Soldier
1F 3–7 Sarugaku-cho
Shibuya-ku, Tokyo
Japan

Freshjive
3–27–3 Jingumae
Shibuya-ku, Tokyo
Japan
www.freshjive.net

Headporter
3–21–112 Jingumae [1st floor]
Shibuya-ku, Tokyo 150–0001
Japan
www.headporter.org

Hysteric Glamour
5–5–3 Minami Aoyama
Minato-ku, Tokyo 107–0062
Japan
www.hystericglmaour.jp

Neighborhood
Kanzaki Building
4–32–7 Jingumae
Shibuya-ku, Tokyo 150–0001
Japan

Original-Fake
Oh Building B1
5–3–25 Minami Aoyama
Minato-ku, Tokyo 107–0062
Japan
www.original-fake.com

Prohibit
2F TF Building
4–31–4 Jingumae
Shibuya-ku, Tokyo 150–0001
Japan
www.prohibitnyc.com

Real Mad Hectic
4–26–21 Jingumae
Shibuya-ku, Tokyo
Japan

Recon
Harajuku Complex 1F
4–29–7 Jingumae
Shibuya-ku, Tokyo 150–0001
Japan
www.reconstore.com

Sarcastic
Harajuku 4–26–27
Jingumae
Shibuya-ku, Tokyo 150–000
Japan
www.sarcasticclothing.com

Silas & Maria
3–13 Daikanyama Cho
Shibuya-ku, Tokyo
Japan
www.silasandmaria.com

Stüssy
7–14 Sakura Ga Oka
Shibuya, Tokyo
Japan
www.stussy.com

Supreme
1–6 Daikanyama-cho
Shibuya-ku, Tokyo 150–0034
Japan
www.supremenewyork.com

Undefeated
2–9–2 Gofuku-cho Aoi-ku
Shizuoka
Japan
www.undftd.com

Undercover
5–3–18 Minami Aoyama
Minato-ku, Tokyo 107–0062
Japan

Visvim (F.I.L)
5–9–17 Jingumae [Level B1]
Shibuya-ku, Tokyo
Japan
www.visvim.tv

MEXICO

Headquarter
Atlixco 118, Col. Condesa
06100 Mexico D.F.
Mexico
www.headquarterstore.com

NETHERLANDS

Patta
Nieuwezijds Voorburgwal 1421012
SH–Amsterdam
Netherlands
www.patta.nl

SINGAPORE

Surrender
14 Scotts Road, #03–06
Far East Plaza
Singapore 228213
Singapore
www.surrenderous.com

SPAIN

Trust Nobody
Carrer dels Tallers, 108001
Barcelona
Spain
www.trustnobody.es

SWEDEN

Cali Roots
Brunnsgatan 9111
38 Stockholm
Sweden
www.caliroots.com

SWITZERLAND

Grandism
Birmensdorfstrasse, 138004
Zürich
Switzerland
www.grandism.com

TAIWAN

Busy Work Shop (BAPE)
1F No. 9 Alley 35,
Lane 181 Sec. 4
Jhongsiao ERD Da-An District
Taipai
Taiwan
www.bape.com

UNITED KINGDOM

Best
No. 5 Back Hill
London EC1R 5EN
United Kingdom
www.bestshopever.com

Bond International
17 Newburgh Street
London W1F 7RZ
United Kingdom
www.bondinternational.com

Busy Work Shop (BAPE)
4 Upper St James Street
London W1F 9DG
United Kingdom
www.bape.com

Cinch
5 Newburgh Street
London W1F 7 RB
United Kingdom

DPMHI
2/3 Great Pulteney Street
London W1F 9LY
Great Britain
www.dpmhi.com

The Duffer of St George
27 D'Arbley Street
London W1
United Kingdom
www.thedufferofstgeorge.com

Foot Patrol
16A St Anne's Court
London W1F 0BG
United Kingdom
www.foot-patrol.com

Gloria's
6 Dray Walk
The Old Truman Brewery
London E1 6QL
United Kingdom
www.superdeluxe.net

Griffin Concept Store
297 Portobello Road
London W10 5TD
United Kingdom
www.griffin-studio.com

Hanon
51 The Green
Aberdeen AB11 6NY
United Kingdom
www.hanon-shop.com

Hideout Store
7 Upper St James Street
London W1F 9DH
United Kingdom
www.hideoutstore.com

Microzine
Colebrook Row
London N1 8AB
United Kingdom
www.microzine.co.uk

One40Five
27 Sydney Street
Brighton BN1 4EP
United Kingdom
www.one40fivestore.com

Slammin' Kicks
37 Beak Street
London W1F9RZ
United Kingdom
www.slamminkicks.com

Stüssy
19 Earlham Street
London WC2H 9LL
United Kingdom
www.stussy.com

The Three Threads
47–49 Charlotte Road
London EC2A 3QT
United Kingdom

UNITED STATES

5 & A Dime
828 G Street,
San Diego CA 92101
United States
www.5andadime.com

A New York Thing
51 Hester Street,
New York NY 10002
United States
www.anewyorkthing.com

Alife Rivington Club
158 Rivington Street
New York NY 10002
United States
www.alifenyc.com

Bodega
6 Clearway Street,
Boston MA 02115
United States
www.bdgastore.com

Brooklyn Projects
2125 West Sunset Boulevard
Los Angeles CA 90026
United States

7664 Melrose Avenue
Los Angeles CA 9004
United States
www.brooklynprojects.com

Busy Work Shop (BAPE)
91 Greene Street
New York NY 10012
United States
www.bape.com

Capitol 1524
1524 East Olive Way
Seattle WA 98122
United States
www.capitol1524.com

Clientele
267 Lafayette Street
New York NY 10012
United States

Commissary
803 F Street
San Diego CA 92101
United States

2981 Bristol Street B6
Costa Mesa CA 92626
United States
www.commissaryoc.com

Commonwealth
727 West 21st Street
Norfolk VA 23517
United States
www.cmonwealth.com

Dave's Quality Meat
7 East 3rd Street
New York NY 10003
United States
www.davesqualitymeat.com

Famous Friends
616 East 9th Street
New York NY 10003
United States
www.famousfriendsnyc.com

Flight Club New York
254 Greene Street
New York NY 10003
United States
www.flightclubnewyork.com

Goods
1112 Pike Street
Seattle WA 98101
United States
www.needgoods.com

Grey One
15 East Holly Street
Pasadena CA 91103
United States
www.greyone.com

HUF
516 Hayes Street
San Francisco CA 94102
United States

808 Sutter Street
San Francisco CA 94109
United States
www.hufsf.com

Kendo
7218 Melrose Avenue
Los Angeles CA 90046
United States
www.kendo-la.com

Kicks
3938 West Sunset Boulevard
Los Angeles CA 90048
United States
www.kickssoleprovider.com

Motive 807
710 Brazos Street
Austin TX 78701
United States
www.motive807.com

Nom de Guerre
640 Broadway
New York NY 10012
United States

88 North 6th Street
Brooklyn NY 11211
United States
www.nomdeguerre.net

Nort
359 Lafayette Street
New York NY 10012
United States

1827 Powell Street
San Francisco CA 94133
United States

Odin
199 Lafayette Street
New York NY 10003
United States
www.odinnewyork.com

Prohibit
269 Elizabeth Street
New York NY 10012
United States
www.prohibitnyc.com

Recon
359 Lafayette Street
New York NY 10012
United States

1827 Powell Street
San Francisco CA 94133
United States
www.reconstore.com

Stüssy
140 Wooster St
New York NY 10012
United States

112 South La Brea Avenue
Los Angeles CA 90036
United States

1409 Haight Street
San Francisco CA 94117
United States
www.stussy.com

Supreme
274 Lafayette Street
New York NY 10012
United States

439 Fairfax Avenue
Los Angeles CA 90036
United States
www.supremenewyork.com

The Reed Space
151 Orchard Street
New York NY 10002
United States
www.thereedspace.com

Ubiq
1509 Walnut Street
Philadelphia PA 19103
United States
www.ubiqlife.com

Undefeated
2654–B Main Street
Santa Monica CA 90405
United States

3827 West Sunset Boulevard
Los Angeles CA 90026
United States

112 1/2 South La Brea Avenue
Los Angeles CA 90036
United States
www.undftd.com

Union
172 Spring Street
New York NY 10012
United States

110 South La Brea Avenue
Los Angeles CA 90036
United States

Unsteady
626 8th Avenue
San Diego CA 92101
United States

WTHN
17 North 3rd Street
Philadelphia PA 19106
United States
www.wthnphla.com

FURTHER READING

This is a list of books that I have found to be inspiring, either because of their subject matter and presentation, or both. It is by no means a complete list of books that are out there, but it does offer a glimpse of the streetwear world accessible via books.

AKA, *Also Known As: Volume 1,* 12oz Prophet/AKA, 2006

Banksy, *Wall & Piece,* Century, 2005

Blechman. H (Ed.), *DPM – Disruptive Pattern Material. An Encyclopaedia of Camouflage: Nature, Military and Culture,* DPM Ltd, 2004

Chalfant, H., and Prigoff, J., *Spraycan Art,* Thames & Hudson 1987

Cliver, S., *Disposable – A History of Skateboard Art,* Warwick Publishing, 2005

Colegrave, S. and Sullivan, C., *Punk,* Cassell Illustrated, 2001

Cooper, M. and Chalfant, H., *Subway Art,* Thames & Hudson, 1984

Downey, L., Novack Lynch, J. and McDonough, K., *This is a Pair of Levi Jeans,* Metropolitan Museum of Art, 2002

Fish, J., *I'm With Stupid,* Umbrella, 2005

Friedman, G. E., *Fuck You Heroes: Glen E. Friedman Photographs, 1976–91,* 2-13-61-U.S., 1994

Futura and Drury, B., *Futura,* Booth-Clibborn Editions, 2000

Ganz, N., *Graffiti World: Street Art from Five Continents,* Thames & Hudson, 2004

Garcia, B., *Where'd You Get Those? New York's Sneaker Culture: 1960–1987,* powerHouse Books, 2003

Grosenick, U., *Art Now,* Taschen, 2005

Hecox, E., *Evan Hecox: drawings, painting and prints,* Arkitip, 2003

Holmes, A. and Prantera, S., *Where Is Silas?,* Laurence King Publishing, 2003

Howell, A., *Art, Skateboarding and Life,* Gingko Press, 2005

James, T., *Todd James (REAS),* Testify Books, 2004

Jones, T. and Jones, T., *Smile i-D Fashion and Style: the Best from 20 Years of i-D,* Taschen, 2001

Klanten, R., *BLK/MRKT ONE*, BLK/MRKT Gallery, 2001

Klanten, R. and Bourguin, N., *Tres Logos*, Die Gestalten Verlag, 2006

Klanten, R., Hellige, H. and Hulan, T. (Eds), *Sonic: Visuals for Music*, Die Gestalten Verlag, 2004

Kronbauer, B., *Beach Glass*, Holy Water, 2004

Maikels, T., *Thrasher – Insane Terrain*, Universe Publishing, 2001

Marcopoulis, A., *Pass The Mic Beastie Boys 1991–1996*, powerHouse Books, 2001

Marcoupolis, A., *Slouching Towards Brooklyn*, Nieves, 2006

Marcoupolis, A., *Under Penalty of Perjury*, Nieves, 2006

Moore, T., *Mix Tape: The Art of Cassette Culture*, Universe Publishing, 2004

Ochs, M., *Classic Rock Covers*, Taschen, 2001

Phunk Studio, *Mono Number One: Phunk Studio*, Die Gestalten Verlag, 2004

Powell, R., *Public Access: Ricky Powell Photographs 1985–2005*, powerHouse Books, 2005

Poyner, R., *Designed by Peter Saville*, Frieze, 2003

Rankin and Hack, J., *Rankin Works*, Booth-Clibborn Editions, 2000

Robertson, M., *Factory Records: The Complete Graphic Album*, Thames & Hudson, 2006

Rose, A., *Dysfunctional*, Booth-Clibborn Editions, 1999

Rose, A. (Ed.), *Young, Sleek and Full of Hell: Ten Years Of New York's Alleged Gallery 1992–2002*, Drago Publications, 2005

Schiffmacher, H., *1000 Tattoos*, Taschen, 2002

Shaughnessy, A., *How to Be a Graphic Designer: Without Losing Your Soul*, Laurence King Publishing, 2005

Shinomiya, C. and Thacker, T. (Eds), *Hot Rods & Custom Cars: Vintage Speed Graphics*, Taschen, 2004

Sola, M., *Proud 2 Be A Flyer: The Historical Roots of A Design Revolution*, Gingko Press, 2004

Steyck, C. and Carson, D., *Surf Culture: The Art History of Surfing*, Gingko Press, 2002

Sutherland, P., *Autograf: New York City's Graffiti Writers*, powerHouse Books, 2004

Templeton, E., *The Golden Age of Neglect*, Drago Arts & Communication, 2002

Unorthodox Styles, *Sneakers: The Complete Collectors' Guide*, Thames & Hudson, 2005

Walters, H., *300% Cotton*, Laurence King Publishing

Wiedermann, J. (Ed.), *Taschen's 1000 Favourite Websites*, Taschen, 2003

Witten, A., *Dondi: Style Master General: The Life and Art of Dondi White*, Harpercollins, 2003

MAGAZINES &
WEB RESOURCES

13th Witness
www.13thwitness.com

A Silent Flute (blog)
http://blog.asilentflute.com

Adiktion Magazine
www.adiktionmag.com

Another Magazine
www.anothermag.com

ANP
www.rvcaanp.com

Aquatelle Magazine
www.aquatulle.com

Arkitip
www.arkitip.com

Being Hunted
www.beinghunted.com

Black Book Magazine
www.blackbookmag.com

Black Rainbow Extraordinaire Magazine
www.bkrw.com

Bob Kronbauer
www.bobkronbauer.com

Boon
www.s-boon.com

The Brilliance
www.thebrilliance.com

Clarks Modart Magazine
www.modarteurope.com

Cliquenmove
www.cliquenmove.com

Clutter Magazine
www.cluttermagazine.com

Code Magazine
www.code-magazine.com

Complex
www.complex.com

Cool Hunting
www.coolhunting.com

Cool Trans
www.cooltransmag.com

Core77
www.core77.com/blog

Crazy Steez
www.nebol.com

Crooked Tongues
www.crookedtongues.com

Dazed and Confused
www.confused.co.uk

Delphi
www.delphicollective.com

Dopefiend
www.dopefiend.ca

Don't Believe the Hypebeast
www.dontbelievethehypebeast.com

The Drama
www.thedrama.org

Educated Community
www.ecnyc.org

Effingdope.com
www.effingdope.com

The Fader
www.thefader.com

Fat Lace Magazine
www.fat-lace.com

Fatsarazzi
www.fatsarazzi.co.uk

Fecal Face
www.fecalface.com

Frank151
www.frank151.com

Freshness Magazine
www.freshnessmag.com

Garage Magazin
www.garagemagazin.net

Giant Robot
www.giantrobot.com

Glob
www.anewyorkthing.com/wp

High Snobiety
www.highsnobiety.com

Honeyee Magazine
www.honeyee.com

Huge
www.kodansha.co.jp/huge

The Hundreds
www.thehundreds.com

Hype Beast
www.hypebeast.com

i-D Magazine
www.i-dmagazine.com

Juxtapoz
www.juxtapoz.com

Lace Magazine
www.lace-mag.de

Lif
www.lifmag.com

Lodown Magazine
www.lodownmagazine.com

Made
www.mademag.com

Mass Appeal
www.massappealmag.com

Milk Magazine
www.milk.com.hk

Morel Works
www.morelworks.com

ODD Magazine
www.oddmagazine.se

Paper Magazine
www.papermag.com

Purple Magazine
www.purple.fr

Relax
http://relax.magazine.co.jp

Rift Trooper's Head Quarters
www.rthq.com

The Royal Magazine
www.theroyalmagazine.com

Slam X Hype
www.slamxhype.com

Sneaker Freaker
www.sneakerfreaker.com

Spine Magazine
www.spinemagazine.com

Style and the Family Tunes
www.stylemag.net

Sup Magazine
www.supmag.com

Superfuture
www.superfuture.com

Super Touch
www.supertouchblog.com

Think Silly
www.think-silly.com/tk

TMI
www.themostinfluential.com/
londonaire.html

Tokion Magazine
www.tokionmagazine.com

Vapors, All City Magazine
www.vaporsmagazine.com

WAD
www.wadmag.com

Warp
www.twj.to

Wooster Collective
www.wooostercollective.com

WRG Magazine
www.whatsreallygoodmagazine.com

ACKNOWLEDGMENTS

First and foremost I would like to thank my wife Nina for her patience, support and understanding, not only in the creation of this book, but also for the path I have chosen to follow (in as much as it has chosen me). Without her, none of this would have happened and I am eternally thankful, and in her debt, for all that she does for me.

I also want to thank all the contributors to this book. Again, without you this would not have been possible and I am grateful for your friendship and support.